More praise for *Oc...*

"Prize-winning novelist Sandra Scofiel... honest memoir of her mother's deat... ...her own attempts, more than four decades later, to go in search of both that beautiful mother and that adoring daughter. . . . In its rapturous Catholicism and its longing for the beloved parents, *Occasions of Sin* resonates with the power of Mary Gordon's search for her father in *The Shadow Man*."

—Shelby Hearon, *Dallas Morning News*

"The events chronicled in *Occasions of Sin* have been churning in Scofield's imagination and ideation for a lifetime, and they moved her primally. We are graced as she attempts to confront their meaning, for she has insight and language strong enough to bring us along. . . . In its groping sense of honesty and its plain-spoken, understated pain, [*Occasions of Sin*] has the attributes of a classic."

—Art Winslow, *Chicago Tribune*

"*Occasions of Sin* is the heart-piercingly beautiful memoir of the childhood and youth of Sandra Scofield, a writer who has been nominated for the National Book Award. It is also the story of Scofield's intense relationship with her mother, a lovely, thoughtful woman trapped in a provincial world, doomed to die young, just as her daughter is becoming a woman. . . . Unlike some recent memoirs that seem to offer something 'extra' beyond the personal narrative (insights into monasticism, thoughts on writing, etc.), this book is truly a pure memoir—which this reader found refreshing. With a small cast of characters and the inexhaustible themes of faith, sex, and family, it reads like a novel—which is precisely what Scofield has built her career writing." —Greg Wolfe, *Image Update*, the online newsletter of *Image: A Journal of the Arts & Religion*

"Four decades have passed since the events that Scofield compellingly narrates, but the reader who appreciates the instructive quality of witnessing the way another person 'exorcises' the past

will find *Occasions of Sin* to be a cathartic and rewarding experience. . . . Scofield's personal story develops the quality of a universal story as the author strives to rediscover the mother she loved deeply but who was lost to her far too early to be understood as deeply as she was loved."
—www.nimblespirit.com, *The Literary Spirituality Review*

"Sandra Scofield, a longtime novelist, brings a literary lushness and a distanced perspective to her memoir. . . . In an era when women were not supposed to want anything for themselves, both Sandra and Edith tried to reconcile their fears and desires and to understand how religion fits into the real world, where occasions of sin seemed to be hovering around every corner."
—Frances Lefkowitz, *Body & Soul*

"There is a steely honesty to this book, in which Scofield confronts the protean nature of a loved one preserved in memory. . . . Maternal memoirs and fiction typically leave the reader comparing actual life with that of the characters—with varying degrees of identification or relief. Not so with this book: Scofield's clear-eyed view rubs off, and we are able to see this as first, and last, Edith's story. It is a privilege to share it."
—Kimberly Marlow Hartnett, Portland *Oregonian*

"One of the year's Best Books: Northwest!!"
—Portland *Oregonian*, December 26, 2004

"Scofield is an accomplished novelist who moves into the memoir genre with grace. . . . Luminous language, together with years of reflection that have obviously led to real retrospective wisdom, make . . . *Occasions of Sin* both graceful and enlightening."
—Judith Barrington, *Women's Review of Books*

"*Occasions of Sin* evokes the complicated and all-consuming nature of Scofield's love for her mother. . . . This uncompromising book does not move toward any tidy moments of acceptance; there is no sunset-cued epiphany in which Scofield realizes that everything will be all right. . . . *Occasions of Sin* succeeds on its own unflinching terms." —Amy Kroin, *Washington Post Book World*

"Scofield layers a detailed, often grim account of the failures and persistence of love. . . . With precision, the mature Scofield seeks to understand her mother's failures and her own ambivalence at establishing a separate identity. . . . Scofield investigates the insistence of desire, the inability to transcend the body and the indissoluble bond between mother and daughter . . . a narrative of survival." —Jean Barber, *San Francisco Chronicle*

"Even in a sea of outstanding memoirs, this one stands out. . . . From the most ordinary of circumstances, the author crafts a riveting, deeply moving story about her West Texas childhood." —John Portmann, *Virginia Quarterly Review*

"There is no trace of untoward ego in this book. There is unrelenting honesty, deep compassion and an overwhelming desire to understand. . . . This book is beautiful, passionate, moving and filled with humor and warmth." —Dan Hays, *Statesman Journal*, Salem, Oregon

"A much-praised Oregon novelist shows her talent for memoir . . . with a finely crafted recollection of her invalid mother growing up Catholic in West Texas four decades ago." —*Seattle Post-Intelligencer*

"A marvelous model of truthful and courageous storytelling, a moving and heartrending narrative about growing up Catholic in a working class family struggling to survive." —Susan Rogers, *Ashland Daily Tidings*

"Scofield takes the reader on her journey of self-discovery. It is her portrait of pure honesty that makes [*Occasions of Sin*] pure pleasure to read." —Mary Trawick, *womenwriters.net*

"A tender but clear-eyed tribute." —*Kirkus Reviews*

"Poignant and clearly cathartic, this is a tender, melancholic coming-of-age story." —*Publishers Weekly*

"[Scofield] is a skilled stylist. . . . [*Occasions of Sin*] explore[s] the mother/daughter relationship with insight and sensitivity."
—*Library Journal*

"This is a deeply reflective and heartrending account of all that is lost when a child loses her mother." —*Booklist*

"Sandra Scofield has written a beautifully evocative memoir that captures the essence of that most mysterious relationship—the one we have with the being that carried us in her body and brought us into the world, our mother. Is there anyone who knows her mother's secrets? . . . This is a rich story, full of love, anger, grief, mistakes, forgiveness and wisdom. It is written with almost shocking honesty but without bitterness or excuses. It left me feeling deeply connected to my own childhood and teen years, grateful to have been reminded." —Carolyn Blankenship, Storycircle.org

"Sandra Scofield writes with exquisite attention to detail, great compassion, and deep honesty. *Occasions of Sin* is a book that to my mind validates memoir as a form: its commitment to storytelling, its perfectly crafted prose, the author's real desire to forgive her mother and to understand her." —Pam Houston, author of *Sight Hound* and *Cowboys Are My Weakness*

"Having spent much of my Catholic girlhood in Texas, I can vouch for how eerily perfect Sandra Scofield gets the details right, from using Necco wafers for 'practice Communion,' to our nerdy, overachiever yearnings for sainthood. But it is the heartbreaking emotional specificity in this exquisitely wrought tale of a forsaken daughter's passionate love for her beautiful mother that gives *Occasions of Sin* its universal appeal." —Sarah Bird, author of *The Yokota Officers Club*, *The Boyfriend School*, and *Alamo House*

"Sandra Scofield has written an aching memoir of a daughter's need for her dying and eccentric mother's love, a complex tale of belief and bonds. She draws us skillfully into this push and pull between a desperate woman and a daughter's desire. This is a tale filled with longing and loss as well as a powerful sense of what it means to be holy and what it is like to sin."

—Mary Morris, author of *Acts of God*

"Sometimes our most private yet vital act of compassion—learning to forgive our younger selves and our families, for the mistakes we made, or the mistakes others made and we endured—takes a lifetime of looking back to achieve, but only then can grace ripen in one's heart, in the fullness of one's life, as it has here in Sandra Scofield's wonderful memoir, with its tender undercurrents of sorrow and luminosity."

—Bob Shacochis, author of *Domesticity* and *Swimming in the Volcano*

"No one understands the vexed relationship between mothers and daughters as well as Sandra Scofield. Written with a compassion tempered by clear-eyed honesty, *Occasions of Sin* is the memoir of a woman who survives her own and her family's trauma to celebrate the magic and mystery of ordinary love. Scofield touches the heart." —Jonis Agee, author of *Acts of Love on Indigo Road*

NOVELS BY SANDRA SCOFIELD

Gringa
Beyond Deserving
Walking Dunes
More Than Allies
Opal on Dry Ground
A Chance to See Egypt
Plain Seeing

OCCASIONS OF *Sin*

· A MEMOIR ·

by SANDRA SCOFIELD

W. W. NORTON & COMPANY
NEW YORK   LONDON

FOR BILL AND JESSICA,

AS ALWAYS,

AND FOR MARY

Copyright © 2004 by Sandra Scofield

For information about permission to reproduce selections from this book,
write to Permissions, W. W. Norton & Company, Inc., 500 Fifth Avenue,
New York, NY 10110

Manufacturing by Quebecor World, Fairfield
Book design by Judith Stagnitto Abbate / Abbate Design
Production manager: Amanda Morrison

Library of Congress Cataloging-in-Publication Data

Scofield, Sandra Jean, 1943–
Occasions of sin : a memoir / Sandra Scofield.— 1st ed.
p. cm.
ISBN 0-393-05735-6 (hardcover)
1. Scofield, Sandra Jean, 1943-—Homes and haunts—Texas, West. 2. Novelists,
American—20th century—Family relationships. 3. Scofield, Sandra Jean, 1943-—
Childhood and youth. 4. Novelists, American—Homes and haunts—Texas, West.
5. Novelists, American—20th century—Biography. 6. Terminally ill parents—Texas,
West. 7. Mothers and daughters—Texas, West. 8. Teenage girls—Texas, West.
9. Catholics—Texas, West. 10. Texas, West—Biography. I. Title.
PS3569.C584Z477 2004
813'.54—dc22

2003018197

ISBN 0-393-32721-3 pbk.

W. W. Norton & Company, Inc., 500 Fifth Avenue, New York, N.Y. 10110
www.wwnorton.com

W. W. Norton & Company Ltd., Castle House, 75/76 Wells Street, London W1T 3QT

1 2 3 4 5 6 7 8 9 0

· AUTHOR'S NOTE ·

This narrative is true, but these are my memories and no one else's. I have changed the names of all individuals outside my family.

I offer my deep respect and gratitude to my editor, Jill Bialosky, and my thanks to her wonderful Norton colleagues; gratitude to my steadfast agent, Emma Sweeney; and abiding love to my aunt, Mae Perkins, for a childhood of summers and all the stories.

OCCASIONS OF *Sin*

Sometime in the weeks before she died in March 1959, my mother, Edith, was photographed in her bedroom in the natural light coming through her window. I have six black-and-white 8 × 10 proofs. She is nude in the photographs except that in two she wears a garter belt, stockings, and high heels. The photographer was our neighbor, a young family man who had a children's portrait studio downtown. I came home in the middle of the day unexpectedly and opened the door on them; he was kneeling on her bed while she stood naked, holding back the filmy curtain with one hand behind her. I assume that the session was her idea, since I cannot imagine the young man suggesting it. She was a frail woman who had been bedridden for most of a year, a wife and mother, and this was a conservative time and place. I doubt that he charged her; the inferior quality of the printing indicates that he didn't feel obliged to give her good prints. The experience of photographing a nude model, and the negatives, were probably his fee.

My mother, who had once been beautiful, was thirty-three years old and had been sick for a long time, retaining fluid and turning pale and puffy with splotches of ocher and blue over her body. The photographs are surprisingly kind to her, dark enough that the dimpling of her skin does not show. In two of them she holds her arms up behind her head, lengthening her torso; in most of them she is coyly looking away or down. Only in the pictures in which she wears stockings, one foot propped on a chair, does she seem uneasy. I think the photographer must have insisted on those shots: *We'll just do a few my way. After all, there is no charge.* The one photograph in which she looks directly at the camera captures a forthright, comfortable gaze, the look of someone who knows she has moved on.

How many times I have studied those pictures, trying to guess what she was thinking. Did she like showing her body to the camera? To the man? To those of us who would see it later? Was she remembering her youth, or did she think she still had that special something? She does not look like a woman anticipating death.

I cannot find a reason why she would want the photographs, why she would give them to me and say, *They're for you,* unless she meant to assert herself at a time when she felt pitiable; yet I know I have projected that rationale onto her. I used to be ashamed of the photographs and of her, but I never threw them away, nor did my grandmother. Neither of us would lose that last glimpse of her.

While I was staying with my grandmother after college, she

took the photograph in which Mother looked at the camera, and she cut my mother's head away from the spectacle of her naked body and she put the head in a frame and set it on a ledge on the living-room wall, as if that would make either of us forget the discarded part. My mother's eyes followed me no matter where I stood in the room, and I could not keep from looking back at her. I came to believe that her expression was the same as the one she gave me when I opened the door and found her posing with her clothes off, bemused, perhaps condescending, the sort of look a mother might give a daughter when she knows the daughter will make too much of a situation.

The photograph, whose display I saw at first as a gesture of loyalty (*We love her no matter what!*), became a reminder of my mother's moral failings, and in some way an accusation of me, a kind of covenant between us, a recognition that I would follow her ways.

My grandmother took everything she could that had been Mother's out of our house but stored it all away in sheds and closets in her own. The only visible keepsakes were the cutout photo and Mother's refrigerator. Even the sweetest photographs of Mother and me from my childhood—snapshots taken at swimming pools, at birthday parties and other family gatherings, dress-up pictures before church on Easter, and so on—were buried in boxes under boxes. We never talked about those times. I believed that my grandmother did not speak of Mother because she thought she had done bad things; all my life I had heard that old admonition *Don't speak ill of the dead*. Slivers of old family talk surfaced in me like festered gossip and slowly I began to remember or to guess what those things had been. This was the girl who had stolen money from her mother to run away at sixteen. It didn't matter that she came back; whatever she had wanted could never be hers.

I did not press my grandmother. I was still clinging to hairs of love and I knew that I was my mother's daughter. I thought what we would say might cast yet a darker shadow over her memory. Her absence was a great cavity we tiptoed around. I no longer admired or even believed in her piety; as my own faith leaked away, so did my loving memory of the mother-daughter rituals attached to it, and in this way I lost another part of her and of myself.

I found a stationery box in the back of a dresser drawer that held half a dozen snapshots of Mother as a young woman. I took them out and studied them covertly, usually in bed late at night. One is only 1 × 2 yet vivid and lovely. She is standing among a profusion of vines against a stucco wall. She wears a checked skirt and white blouse and dark cardigan, looking like a schoolgirl in bright sunlight. I know now that the picture was taken just before she realized she was pregnant with me.

In another, she sits in profile, wearing a two-piece bathing suit and high heels. Little by little I grew to dislike it as over-posed and somehow representative of something I could not quite name. Her feet are crossed; she leans back, propped on her extended arms; she smiles, sure that the camera loves her. This glamour shot was taken on the rickety wooden porch of my grandmother's tiny stucco house on North Lamar in Wichita Falls, Texas; just below my mother is the clumsy concrete slab that served as a step, and an overturned, mud-crusted jar. She is eighteen, poor, and trapped (I am already nearly a year old); her beauty isn't worth a dime. *Who does she think will see her?*

Those photographs—she is so pretty, and so hopeful, whatever angry criticism I conjured—inspired my imagination. I didn't know what I was doing, but now I see that I needed a way to encapsulate my mother, a way to carry her around inside me, and the ways you would think of—photograph albums, family stories—had been suppressed, and I didn't have the right words. I had only fragments, hints of secrets, and my own troubled adolescent history to draw on, so I shaped a story that was about sin and abandonment, perfectly twisting her beauty to my slant. She had been a spoiled and needy child who grew up using everyone else's resources. She always wanted *more*. Her vanity kept her from seeing how limited her prospects were, and it made her extravagant. Her piety had been all tied up with priests and her own self-interests. She had seduced her doctor and cast out her husband. Worst of all, she had not taken proper care of herself, nor of us, and she had died. She had given up (the best version) or maybe died by her own hand.

There you have it. I thought it was a sign of maturity to admit the truth: The life my mother led used up everyone around her and still failed to give her what she wanted.

I could see myself doing bad things, too. I thought sin was a one-way street; I didn't believe in redemption. Proof was in the past. She had tried for years to be holy and look what happened. Hadn't she died in sin?

I cringe to think of myself judging her. It has taken me a long time to understand that my memories largely shape the meaning of my life, and that sometimes memories are a trick you play on yourself. When you lose your mother at a young age, you lose a part of who you are; you spend years navigating what amounts to chaos without any sort of reliable compass. The more bewildered and ashamed you are, the more you avoid reflection, the more you lash out—it's always someone else's fault. The past is a site of great injustice, the place where your parents failed you; the place where you see, nonetheless, the only possibility for connection. Sometimes, parked in a car with a boy who hardly knew me, I would wonder what my mother would say if she could see us. I went from worrying about doing the wrong thing to striving for it. *You're not the only one!* I might have been screeching to heaven. Now, when sex is freely discussed with good humor and no embarrassment in print, on film, and among friends and strangers, I don't know which amazes me more: this present easiness, or the memory of just how serious it once seemed to me. How much I lost, giving it away, when I thought it was a sin.

Why, when my mother was buried, was her *person* forgotten? Why did no one give me reason to admire her, my mother, my model? We never spoke of her accomplishments or her dreams (for her children, more than for her), never gave her credit for her passion and her striving.

Did no one stop to think that I might turn out just like her, *just like I thought she was?*

ONE

Becoming Catholic was one of Mother's notions. A "notion" set her apart from her hard-working kin; it was an impulse that sprang from eccentricity, a torque in her self-perception. She didn't seem to know who she was. She had always been poor. Her father, Ira, had plowed fields with a mule, then was killed by a dust devil (a transient whirlwind) in 1936, and her mother, Frieda, had lived in a boxcar and cooked for railroad gangs until the country entered World War II and factory jobs opened for women. Mother had dropped out of school at fourteen and lied about her age in order to become a Harvey Girl (a waitress) in Winslow, Arizona. In Wichita Falls, she had worked as a drugstore clerk and café waitress and at a drive-in called the Pig Stand, locally famous for its barbecue and pretty carhops. Even though she was married and had two children at the time of her conversion, she was living in her mother's cramped house because her young husband, Dean Hupp, couldn't provide reliable support. Yet she had a rampant dream life and a vivid sense of herself in another kind of world entirely. She had an imagination, she read novels and poetry. It was a short leap to religion.

She brought art books home from the library and taught me the names of famous painters and sculptors. She wrote poetry and drew. Once she took in kids for day care and taught them to count from one to ten in Spanish and French. She loved fashion. She would spend half a day trying on clothes, then put a beautiful dress on layaway that she would never have occasion to wear; often as not, she lost her deposit. She spent idle hours sketching dresses sized to fit the distorted models illustrated in the *Frederick's of Hollywood* lingerie catalogs. (My efforts alongside her were my first lessons in drawing.) I was a toddler when she spent a season working box office for the community theater, hauling me along so I would be around creative people. She volunteered with the local Democratic precinct, where her talent for organization shone, and for a little while she dreamed of becoming an attorney's assistant (despite her lack of education), but her health held her back. She perplexed the family with her rages during the McCarthy hearings and her deep depression when the Rosenbergs were executed, matters they considered the business of Yankees.

At sixteen she had fancied herself an actress and had struck out to California by train, only to come home sick and defeated, without a word of contrition. She flitted out there again the year I was five, stayed two weeks, and returned by plane, her arrival an event we all treated as if she were returning royalty. I remember perfectly that her purple shoes matched her broad-brimmed hat.

Odd as it was, Mother's conversion had a certain appeal for my grandmother. It might settle her down. No one in the family had actually ever known a Catholic. My grandmother had been raised Lutheran by her German mother, but by the time I could notice such things she had mostly stopped attending church, except when she accompanied her mother. Her father-in-law was a Methodist minister in Chickasha, Oklahoma. Mother and her sister, Eula Mae, and her brother, Louis (Sonny), had attended Methodist services as children, and Mother remembered it as a stuffy religion. Culturally, nothing about her life hinted of the Romans. All of my grandmother's neighbors in her poor section of town were hard-shell Baptist, Church of Christ, or Pentecostal, people who believed Catholics worshiped idols and owed political allegiance to Rome, but Mother would never have joined a shanty religion that dunked its members in stale water stored under the church floorboards or in dirty outdoor ponds.

In the spring of 1950 she spent a couple of weeks in the Catholic hospital in Wichita Falls. She was twenty-four. (Daddy was twenty-three.) I was six, Karen was three, and we were all living in my grandmother's house, maybe 600 square feet, a yellow stucco box on an unpaved street. Mother had been working for a while at the Pig Stand, wearing short shorts and a peasant blouse, her hair in pigtails like a teenager's. One night she came in late, just after my grandmother had returned home from the swing shift at General Mills, where she packed flour in huge cloth sacks. She went into the bathroom to wash up and suddenly she cried out. My grandmother ran into the bathroom and locked the door. They seemed to be in there forever. I stood outside listening to Mother's cries trail off to whimpers and gasps. Daddy stumbled up out of sleep, stepping on the bottom of his too-long pajamas. He stood with his hot palm on the top of my head, waiting until my grandmother opened the door and ordered him to wake up the next-door neighbor and borrow his car to take Mother to the hospital. There was a little pool of blood on the bathroom floor, and I began to cry, but our neighbor Ruth came over in her bathrobe to take Karen and me back to her house for the rest of the night.

Eventually I learned that Mother had "lost a baby" and that she had been warned that another pregnancy, a strain on her kidneys, might kill her. The problems with her kidneys had been identified when she was pregnant with my sister while we were living in Martins Ferry, Ohio, where Daddy, like his father, worked for Railway Express. She had spent most of that pregnancy in bed. My grandmother went up on the train and brought me back to Wichita Falls to ease Mother's burden. (I have letters that Mother wrote my grandmother complaining about my temper fits.) When Karen was a few months old, my grandmother took me back to Ohio. She refused to spend even one night there; she handed me over at the station and turned right around and got back on the train to get off at the next stop and head home. She said she couldn't stand to leave me, and staying would make it harder. (Again, from letters. I'd never invent such a thing.)

It was only a matter of months before Mother and Daddy packed us up and returned to Frieda's crowded house in Texas. Mother went in and out of sieges of anger at her mother all her life, but my grandmother's door was always open and she could always be summoned.

The fact that Mother had a miscarriage explains why she made them take her to the Catholic hospital, where they would not have performed a hysterectomy unless her life were in danger. She must have still dreamed of more children, though she could barely take care of the two she had. Twenty-four is young to lose that possibility.

The hospital wouldn't let children visit, and my grandmother worked a brutal schedule at General Mills. She traded with other "mill girls," as they called themselves, so that she could stay on day shift until Mother came home. Still in her flour-dusted work clothes, a cotton cloth wrapped around her head, she peeked in at the hospital room after work, then hurried home to my sister and me. She always said Mother was looking much better and sent her love.

Without Mother as a buffer, Daddy tried to avoid my grandmother, who never spoke to him and referred to him as "he," never by name. (This was true of men in general.) He had started picking up night shifts with a cab company. He worked occasional day labor, too, with idleness to shame him when there was no work to be had. We girls spent a lot of time next door at the greengrocer's house, where there were daughters our same age to play with and my tow-headed baby sister was especially favored by their mother, Ruth. We ate and bathed there, took naps, and sat politely listening as Ruth read to us from *The Children's Book of Bible Stories*.

Mother was alone at the hospital except for roommates, who came and went. She was still quite beautiful then, with thick, lustrous blond hair and creamy white skin. She was not much more than a girl trapped in a grown-up's life without the taste for it or the stamina, either; she was trembling with longing for something larger than her life. No wonder she fell gratefully under the chaplain's spell. He lavished her with perfectly proper attention, a conduit for God's love.

Father Knopf was a kindly, fiftyish, well-educated Benedictine priest who knew a likely convert when he met her. It took only a couple of conversations for him to recognize her intelligence and her hunger for meaning and solace. I have a clipping of his obituary from a few years later, and in the photograph his sweetness is apparent. Mother took me with her to visit him numerous times after she left the hospital and he always went to the trouble to find paper and a pencil for me, or one of the children's books he kept on hand. He had a warm sense of humor and was fatherly without being patronizing. Once I made up a poem for him, dictated to Mother, something along the lines of *Mary Mother, dressed in blue/ I send a prayer up to you./ Watch my mother, keep her well/ save the sinners all from hell.* He made a nice fuss about it. He was soft-spoken and endlessly patient and he liked to play cards. (Indeed, his zest for the card game Canasta, and the fact that he was German, quite won over my grandmother, who welcomed his visits to the house and kept a beer or two on hand for just such occasions. At seven I became a whiz at Canasta and would happily play for hours as my grandmother's partner against Mother and the visitor priest.)

Each thing he learned about Mother brought him back soon with the perfect pamphlet or book of spiritual reading. I can see it: He pulls up a chair close to her bed and takes her hand. He can't help noting her bitten nails and torn cuticles. The minute she feels the warmth of his clasp, she lets go of the hard tension in her chest, spilling tears, maybe even sobbing. *Why? Why?*

He reaches into his pocket deep in the side of his cassock and extracts a snowy-white handkerchief and tenderly pats her cheeks. "Now, now," he says. "Would you like me to read to you?"

She smiles wanly and he intones prayers from a well-worn

book, its leather cover soft as a glove. He says the things she needs to hear, words that make of her suffering a gift to her Savior, who was both God and man—a man, at that, who understood the power of metaphor.

"A parable," Father says, "is a kind of poem, now isn't it?"

Then he says, "I'll be back in the morning, dear Edith. I'll bring you something to read. We'll talk, all you like." And she pulls her head up from the pillow: "Yes!" she says. How she hungers for talk! "There are so many things I want to ask."

In the morning, a surprise: He brings a book of poetry, miniature size; he has earmarked Donne. And no matter if she doesn't understand. She reads until she knows passages by heart, as one learns a song. Later, he brings her Gerard Manley Hopkins.

Was this the first time she felt that someone took her seriously? The first time that she could open her heart, not for the love of the body, but for love of the soul? No question was silly or over-reaching. God loved her and Father Knopf was his agent. First there was the balm of his sympathy and affection and the flattering attention to her intelligence; then came the recognition of such rightness in the Roman Catholic dogma—the church of great minds. John of the Cross, he of the long, dark night of the soul, something Mother thought she was surely living. Teresa of Avila, who went out there and *did* things. Augustine, first a scoundrel and then a saint. Thomas Merton, a man who could be both cloistered and of the world. To balance the intellectualism, there was the sweetness of Jesus and of his mother. And after a while, there was Thomas à Kempis, and Ignatius Loyola's *Spiritual Exercises*, to which she would return over and over in the years to come. A whole life *within*.

You must abandon yourself to His goodness. Father must have said something like that. Perhaps he read from Saint John Baptist de la Salle, admonishing her to let God decide when her suffering would ease, freeing her from the burden of feeling that she had to try harder to be well. *God will not allow you to be tried beyond your strength.*

What he offered was appealing, tender, and explanatory of her suffering. The nature of her desirability changed, too. Even if her body betrayed her, puffing up and failing, her soul would remain wholesome and radiant. After her discharge from the hospital, Father Knopf delivered her personally to the pastor of Saint Michael's parish. Father Daly (soon to be Monsignor), another gentle man of great intelligence and dignity, and quite handsome besides, instructed and baptized her quickly, and the rest of us soon followed, because that was what she wanted.

First, though, she took the bus to Subiaco, Arkansas, to Father Knopf's home base, the monastery where she would pour her heart out to the abbot, and that good man would write her for years, his letters full of what were by now familiar admonitions to be patient and to put her fate in God's hands. She spent a week in retreat with other women, some of them widows who were thinking of joining religious communities of women. She returned laden with books and holy cards, rosaries and candles. And fudge.

There was more. Embracing Catholicism gave Mother the key to her children's better education and a route for her, like politics would be a little later, to a sense of belonging to something that mattered. She tried to be useful, volunteering for the Altar Society and at the school, but she was undependable, through no fault of her own, and Father Daly taught her that each of us gives what we can. From her, it was the intensity of her devotion and her patience with illness. Indeed, being sick became her identity despite fluctuations and bursts of energy that didn't last. Disappointments were her special blessings and she surrendered to them. In return she was rewarded with welcome at the rectory's side door (*Tap tap* and she would open the screen: *It's me!*). She took her suffering and her longing to Father Daly and he listened and blessed her. Often I met her there after school and sat with the housekeeper having a snack while I waited.

Daddy agreed to meet with Father Daly to talk about his responsibilities to my sister and me and to the Church. Scrubbed and awkward in freshly ironed cotton pants, he headed off with her to the rectory, where he agreed to let Mother raise us Catholic. *You betcha.* What was it to him how his children worshiped? He thought of two things, money and sleep; there was never enough of either. He not only agreed to the stipulations about Karen and me, he agreed to be baptized himself. His explanation was that he might as well get on board. He had to endure evening instruction with a small group of other men, but at least he was out of Frieda's house. He was baptized with Karen and me and sometimes received Communion, but before long his religious practice was reduced to Christmas and Easter. I'm sure that Mother's funeral Mass was the last time he ever set foot in a church. Once I asked him if he had ever really had any interest in it. He chuckled and said, "Not on your life." He wasn't interested in higher things. He had always thought Mother was kidding herself.

. . .

My grandmother lived on a dirt street that flooded fast in hard rains like a desert arroyo. Behind her house in the alley, deep potholes teemed with tadpoles. On hot nights the air flickered with fireflies. Karen and I played with the neighbor girls in their huge sandpile built around a shady tree. I loved the perfume of the honeysuckle that climbed the trellis by their porch. The only rule was that Karen and I couldn't come bare-chested wearing only bloomers, our usual summer costume.

On hot evenings after the sun had set, I played outdoors, games like whip, and Mother, may I? and hopscotch, and hide-and-seek. There were kids in every house, and we clustered and roamed a couple of blocks each way on North Lamar like a pack of puppies, stinking of insect repellent and sweat. There was one girl who could not play with us. She lived across the wide, dirt street from my grandmother a few houses down, and she often sat on her porch steps, her chin on her knees, and watched us. She lived with her grandparents, who were very strict. They were what we called "Holy Rollers." They did not allow music, dancing, or movies. Once I asked if I could play with her in her house, but her grandmother shooed me away with a dishrag like a pesky animal. I was wearing shorts and a halter top, baring my midriff. (I was five.) I still remember what she said: "Shame on your mother. Put some clothes on."

The granddaughter was allowed out of the house only for school and church, and once in a while to walk to the little grocery store for milk or bread. Sometimes, if I saw her coming off the porch into her yard, I ran to the corner away from her house to join her, happy to walk along, scuffing the toes of my shoes in the dirt. Lots of small children were sent to the store clutching a note and a dollar bill or a couple of quarters. No one would have been afraid of abductions. Our area of the city felt like a village. I liked to walk the four or five blocks to the dime store, where I bought packets of powdered candy that tasted like Jell-O; you poured the colored powder in your palm and licked it. Once I offered some to the girl, but she refused it. She said she was not allowed to eat, except at meals.

I asked about her mother, and she said that she had a disease that made her all wobbly, and so she lived in a sort of hospital in Fort Worth. They drove down to see her once every two months. At first her mother had been able to get around with crutches, and then she was in a wheelchair, and then she was, said this girl, "too much to handle." Perhaps it was multiple sclerosis that robbed this girl of her mother.

I asked my mother what she knew about the girl, whose name, I think, was Margaret. I never asked about the father; his absence did not strike me as remarkable. What I did not understand was why the mother was so far away, kept care of by strangers; and why Margaret, a nice girl a year or so older than I, was not allowed to play like the rest of us. None of this lined up with the way things were in my life, though I knew that some other people had strange habits and rules.

Families in our neighborhood were mostly what we would now call the working poor—employed, respectable, and proud. They were also deeply religious. Children called most adults by their last names, and said "ma'am" and "sir." In Texas in those years, everything shut down on Sunday except for restaurants after church. People spoke of God's will the way they spoke of the weather, something hovering or moving in like a cold front. You certainly didn't question it. One block over was a girl with a cleft palate.

Mother said what was awful was that the parents believed it was a special mark from God and would not fix it, even when a service organization would have paid for it. There were children-—mostly boys, but not all—whose fathers beat them with belts and said it was for their own good; on summer nights, when the windows were open, you could hear their shouts and squeals. We would stop our playing and turn toward the sounds, then take up our games again, filling the air with our own screams and laughter. Three lots over, on the corner, there was an anomalous white house, large and colonnaded like a Southern mansion, with a vast, stickerless lawn. The people there owned buildings all over colored town. They had come, my grandmother said, when this neighborhood was just empty prairie. She snickered, "Short-sighted of them to keep so little land." She hated rich people. There were rumors that before we kids were born, the owner had shot a little boy for coming onto his lawn after dark. He got away with it because he was defending his property. True or not, it was our very own boogeyman warning. None of us ever saw the man come or go. The garage was on the distant side, out of our sight. In broad daylight, we dared one another to venture onto the slick green grass. We lined up like border guards and stuck our toes over the edge, then pulled them back in a hurry. My grandmother found me there once and slapped my bottom. She said I might just as well pretend there was a fence as high as the Empire State Building in New York City, the highest building in the world, and *steer clear*.

Mother said that Margaret's strange family likely believed that Margaret's mother had been stricken with disease because she was a sinner. A what? I asked. A wicked person. I was stunned. What could her mother have done to be punished like that? Mother drew me onto her lap and stroked my hair, her lips close to my brow. She said, "A child would sooner have a sick mother than no mother at all."

I suppose Margaret was an illegitimate child, brought home by her mother to raise and then, with the worst of luck, abandoned by her mother's illness. I did not know about unwed mothers and bastard offspring. I thought Margaret's mother was probably a thief; I thought maybe the story was a cover-up for the fact that she was in jail. I didn't know about any other kinds of crimes.

These topics—God's will, sin, and punishment—were still mysterious to me. I knew nothing of God except that the name kept coming up. "Why don't you believe?" the little girls next door asked us. One day they badgered us until Karen ran home wailing. "I *believe* I'll have some iced tea," I said haughtily, trailing after my sister, pulling off my skimpy little top and wiggling my bottom. "I *believe* we might have some yellow cake left."

In time we moved out of my grandmother's house, and she had a frame house built in the newer part of town, and I forgot everyone we left behind. By then I had a religious vocabulary of a sort and a sense of superiority that we had become Catholic. Catholics did not beat their children or lock them in the house, so far as I knew.

KAREN WAS STILL A BABY, but I was ready for school that fall of 1950. In fact, I was a year overdue, a truant. I had started first grade at the public school in August 1949, a couple of weeks after I turned six, but I hadn't lasted long. On that first day, I had thrilled to the sight of the desks in orderly rows. I stood in the doorway, clutching my little bag of sharpened pencils, Crayola crayons, erasers, snub-nosed scissors, and white glue. I was wearing a new dress, pale blue with a stiff, starched skirt and a big bow that tied in the back. Mother had set my hair in tight pin curls the night before, then brushed it into a frowsy fluff caught with two barrettes. I was supposed to line up in the school yard, but she whisked me into the building so that we could see my classroom. She licked her fingers and brushed my thick eyebrows into place. She kissed me on my forehead and touched my lips with her index fingers. "My big girl," she said, and left.

I was eager to get this school thing going. I knew how to read, print simple text, and do basic adding and subtracting. I knew most of the states' capitals and how to measure ingredients for a devil's food cake. I knew about the Statue of Liberty, the Sistine Chapel, and the South Pole. I could identify at least twenty countries on a world map. I expected to learn more complicated things in school, more important things, and maybe to draw better, and sing songs. But as I grew accustomed to the light in the room, I noticed a large chart propped on an easel in the front of the room, and I was suddenly alarmed and sick to my stomach. DICK AND JANE. From where I stood, I saw the sentences, so simple, it wasn't necessary to read the words at all. You simply took them in, like a stop sign. I approached the front of the room and read aloud. *What else?* I thought, knowing instinctively that this was it for first-graders. Behind me someone bustled in. The teacher. She rushed up to me and said crossly, *You stop that right now! We haven't learned to read yet in here. Now you get in line outside where you belong!* She pinched my sleeve.

I suffered through that first day, hardly looking up, but I never returned. Mother must have tried to change my class. I'm sure she went to the principal. Who knows what the options were in 1949?

All I know is that she took me out of school and I spent the rest of the year at home, just as I had the year before, playing, reading, drawing with her. I remember she taught me rudimentary perspective, using two fences converging in the distance. I went everywhere with her. We went to the library every week, taking two buses and splitting a grilled-cheese sandwich at a soda fountain downtown. She read children's books from the library to me until I could read them back, and when she was bored with that, we read from the novels she had chosen for herself. I remember *Ramona,* a novel by Helen Jackson. With construction paper, we made a long worm with a snail's head and stripes, and taped it up across the living room wall. Between the lines I wrote the names of the library books I read, one by one, through the year, until worms ran around the room and into the kitchen.

I can't imagine how she got away with it. She had to have made up a good lie to keep the truant officer at bay once I had been registered. Maybe my grandmother told them we had moved away, back to Ohio or some other state. I do know this: Somehow, in my little girl's brain, I caught on that if the provisions for ordinary people didn't suit me, I could just walk away. Mother would arrange something else.

I was happy to escape and confident in my mother's power to make my life suit us both. I thought we would go on like this forever.

Becoming Catholic, though, was the ticket to something better.

WE WENT TO THE Academy of Mary Immaculate (AMI, we called it) in September. School had been in session for a couple of weeks. Mother explained my history, and of course told them she had just converted. I had not yet been baptized, but it was coming soon. Instead of placing me in first grade, they took me to the second-grade teacher, who handed me a book and asked me to read to her. She put me in her class the next morning. By the end of the day I had been moved to third grade. That night I took my reader home with a crisp manila book cover I folded carefully about the book. Then I lay in bed and finished reading it before I went to sleep. I couldn't believe how easy it was, *third grade*. It took the teacher a few days to figure me and my reading out, but when she did, she was neither pleased nor displeased; she said I didn't need to be in class at reading time, and she would find something else for me to do.

The sisters were capable of adjusting their instruction; they simply moved us around to suit the circumstances, whether up or down. I spent the year going to the library during reading time. Early on, I was joined by a redheaded boy, Denny McMurtry, who would be my companion and rival all my grade-school years. (Mozelle Chambers trumped us in spelling, but we shared first-place honors, later on, in regional piano auditions, standardized test scores, and special projects.) We read what appealed to us. If something struck my fancy, I looked up all I could find on the subject, and constructed elaborate books with illustrations, diagrams, charts, and captions. Mother helped me bind them with strips of leather woven through punched holes.

I woke up every morning elated and came home bursting with news. I liked morning Mass and the donuts and cocoa afterwards in the school basement, and I liked wearing the navy skirt and white camp shirt of our uniform. I liked the sisters and my lessons, and riding the city bus home at the end of the day like a big kid. Even lunch was great, cooked by students' mothers.

Mother always had a snack ready for me as I came in the house. She liked to hear everything about my day. I hated milk but would drink it flavored with powders that came in small packets: banana, strawberry, cherry, chocolate. She was always trying to fatten me up with iced graham crackers, slices of ham, deviled eggs, my grandmother's bread slathered with butter. She said I was a stick. In later years she worried that something was stunted in my development and she took me to doctors to check me over, like a prize calf that didn't grow. I think she was afraid that I would turn out weak like her.

Being Catholic added a whole new slate of activities. Mother and I went to Rosary on Wednesday nights. We went to breakfast in the church hall after Sunday Mass, and got to know other families. We wore little woolen squares on strings around our neck, called scapulars, and bought hats for Sunday Mass. What I liked best about our new, improved life, though, was private: Mother and I praying together in our room before bed.

We girls would bathe and dress in our pajamas and maybe read a book or color for a while at the kitchen table. Then Mother sat on Karen's cot while she said, "Now I lay me down to sleep . . ." and a Hail Mary. Then Karen slept. If Daddy wasn't at work or already asleep, he might be reading Mickey Spillane mysteries in the kitchen. On warm nights, he sat on the back step until everything was quiet and dark indoors. In the summer I liked to take a Mason jar and he would help me catch fireflies. If my grandmother was on night shift, he might make pralines or divinity, using recipes from Mother's cookbook. Sometimes he and Mother played cards. When Mother called me in to bathe, he'd say go on in, he'd sit a while. Sometimes I was still awake on my cot when he came indoors and slipped into bed with Mother. There were whispers, the rustle of the covers and then quickly it was quiet. They had no privacy at all, and with us girls in the room, all was circumspect. Mother and I had more privacy with our prayers.

Praying was like appearing in a play night after night. I had such a strong sense of someone watching, I assumed I was feeling God in the room. I imagined him to be someone a lot like Father Daly, our pastor, only with infinite powers, like a car that never ran out of gas.

Mother had cleared one side of her dresser, an old-fashioned one with a huge round mirror and a place to scoot up a stool in the middle. Each night, she put out holy cards in cheap frames, and lit blessed candles. Kneeling to say the Rosary, I caught glimpses of myself in the mirror and straightened my spine, the better to send my prayers straight up to Heaven. We said the Rosary and then, with us huddled close together on her bed, Mother read stories of martyred saints to me. I found the gruesome ones especially inspiring: beheadings, flayed skin, hot coals, nails in the head. I shuddered at the thought of their anguish. How could they bear it? Why did it have to be so terrible? Mother said that God helped them to stand the onset of pain, then he turned it into something blissful, a joining together with him that taunted their persecutors. She said faith made the martyrs powerful. She said they wouldn't have suffered very long; God made adrenaline shoot through their bodies like a painkiller, frustrating their tormentors. Death was their victory. I loved the idea of standing something on its head that way.

When I was preparing for my First Communion in the spring of that first year at AMI, she impressed on me the solemnity of what I was doing. There was a great fuss in the weeks prior to the festive Mass, when forty of us would march down the aisle and kneel at the marble rail and take this giant step. I had a beautiful white dress and veil, short lace gloves, and a crown that curved like a halo. The white stood for my virginity, which I thought was a special kind of goodness, something I had not lived long enough to soil; and I knew, from the saints' lives, that virgins were God's favorites. I even remember that I felt a little sorry for my mother, who when I asked said no, she wasn't a virgin anymore. She said that sometimes married women became sisters in their later lives, when they were widowed, or their children were grown and did not need their mothers, and the husbands let their wives go to the greater good. She told me about the women she had met at Subiaco Abbey. She sighed. "Those women are never in the inner cloisters, of course, but they are a great help to the community. They are the Marthas."

I didn't yet know about Martha, but I thought, with an icy stab to my chest, that my mother might have preferred that life to the one she had, the one in which I had to be coaxed to eat, had to be driven around, clothes bought, hair brushed, doctors visited. I realized all in a rush that my mother had lost something important because of me, a chance to choose a better path, and I vowed right then to make it worth her while to be my mother. I thought I could take on what she had lost, a vocation. It was a vague concept, yet it weighed in like ore. Whatever prayers we said together I doubled, saying them alone, until I fell asleep.

THE BIG DAY ARRIVES. Mother brushes my hair and smooths Vaseline jelly on my lips. I want a drink of water, but I can neither eat nor drink before Communion. We sit side by side on the bed, waiting for it to be time to go. The bedroom door is closed. She slides to the floor, kneeling beside me, her hands on my legs under my stiff lacy skirt. She looks up at me and smiles. I am licking my lips over and over again. Am I so thirsty? she asks. Tears well in my eyes. It's all I can think about.

She raises up and kisses me. She swishes saliva in her mouth, then licks my lips. I slide my tongue out to take that bit of moisture. I taste the petroleum jelly, and Mother's waxy lipstick.

MAYBE IT IS HARD to believe that I remember this scene so well, but how could I forget it? It was the most important day of my life so far. You would have thought I was about to ascend to Heaven on a cumulus cloud; the formal steps to this day were designed to impress me, and they did. Mother just took all that a little further. From her I was about to learn that God and love, religion and sex (not a word we spoke aloud) are inextricably bound. It wouldn't do, later on, to think of my body in an overly secular, earthly way, since the Church had specific plans for it. I was to be a vessel for Christ now. It was like learning a second language, bit by bit, not by studying, but by paying attention. Comprehension came, not word by word, but whole.

Don't think for a moment that I am ridiculing this rite of passage, my initiation into a profound liturgical mystery. I recall even now the words of Saint Thérèse of Lisieux, writing about her first Communion. My mother read them to me the morning of my own. "Ah! How sweet was that first kiss of Jesus!"

As I read her tender, slightly hysterical writing now, I am struck by its sense of individual entitlement. Like me, Thérèse had been much favored and coddled, especially after her mother's early death. Like my mother, Thérèse seems to have embraced the concept of a private Christ in her, the metaphor made literal—the kind of attitude that lent itself to an oddly visceral interpretation. Catholic children were taught that Christ was physically present to us, as we to him, but no one expected us to take that too far. At that stage of our lives, our religious instruction was purely rote. All I had to do was present myself, open my mouth, and take. Already I was a good female. The celebration of the Eucharist was my introduction to romance and self-love. It was all about Christ, and me, me, me.

"YOU CAN'T IMAGINE what it's like," Mother said. "No matter what you've thought, it will surprise you." She touched her mouth, her throat, she spread her fingers against her chest. Her intensity was contagious. I thrilled with anticipation.

"You will receive the body of Christ," she said. I had heard all of this in my preparation classes. It didn't actually mean much—I was, after all, seven years old. Communion was a round wafer of unleavened bread. The Host. In those days, we did not partake of the Communion wine.

"You don't chew it," she said. I knew that too. I had already practiced. I had taken a thin piece of soft bread crust and put it in my mouth and waited for it to dissolve. It had turned gooey and stuck to the roof of my mouth and finally I had to run my tongue around to scrape it off so that I could swallow. The Host wouldn't be messy like that. It was hardly more than a sliver of milky light. My teeth would never touch it.

She took both my hands and bent her head to kiss them.

"He enters your body," she whispered. *"In His flesh."* His flesh. This is what I mean. Maybe I hadn't heard her exactly right. Maybe I didn't know what she meant, and then again, maybe I did.

Like a tapeworm, I thought.

"Mother?"

"Inside you."

My ears were buzzing. I saw that this was going to be something new between my mother and me, something we wouldn't share with Daddy or my grandmother or even the priests. Jesus' body inside mine. This miracle that happened to my mother every time she went to Mass was going to happen to me, too, even though I was a child, because I was her child. Mother was welcoming me to her side of the experience.

I slithered out of her embrace and stood up. I fluffed my hair, my veil, my stiff skirt. I twirled and gave her a dazzling smile. There are many photographs of me from that time. I knew how to smile for the camera, for the occasion, for the admiration. I had no sense of myself as a child. I'm not convinced any child does. And I didn't have a very good sense of the boundary between my mother and me.

"I can't wait," I said.

. . .

Mother didn't quite make it through that school year.

A friend from the Pig Stand came by, Liz. Mother was happy to see her. Liz had a better job now, at a restaurant. Mother picked up some shifts there on the weekend. She and Liz got together a couple of times a week. Liz didn't have a car; she would suddenly appear at the door and she and Mother would huddle in the bedroom or else stroll down the street toward the bus stop. I'd stay awake as long as I could, but on those nights we didn't fit our prayers in, I knelt by my cot and prayed that Mother would remember her own prayers when she came in.

One day Liz appeared with her things stuffed in paper sacks. When my grandmother came home from the midnight shift, Liz was asleep on the couch. Mother and my grandmother talked it over in the bathroom. Liz had a black eye. She needed a place, just for a few nights.

Liz's husband showed up a couple of nights later while my grandmother was at the mill. Daddy was home and he yelled through the door, *We've called the cops! You go on now!* while the husband banged on the door, cursing and calling Liz's name. Everyone went back to bed. He came again; this time my grandmother was home, and she said Liz had to go, didn't she have kin? Didn't she have other friends? Her husband was a crazy man, and Liz was no one we all ought to be in danger for. Liz wept and Mother wept too, and Liz said she'd clear out the next day, but she didn't. She had turned the couch around so the back of it faced the main part of the room; you could walk through from the front door to the kitchen and not see her sleeping. She had her makeup in a plastic bowl that sat on the floor beside the bathtub, under the window. She went back to work, and brought home groceries and sometimes a couple of bottles of beer. She sat in the kitchen in her slip, telling Mother the story of her life. Her husband found out the phone number and called, day and night, until my grandmother changed her number. She said Liz had to go. That very night someone drove by in a pickup truck with a bad muffler; the driver blared his horn as he drove back and forth. Daddy was away from the house. Liz said she would call the cops, of course it was her husband, but my grandmother said the police weren't going to come to look into somebody driving by honking his horn.

Early in the morning before it was light a car slowed down in front of the house. Something about it scared Liz. She ran back to wake Mother and while she was out of the room there was a shotgun blast through the door, then the car sped away. The police came and wrote down everything Liz told them. They said she'd have to come down later and file a complaint. When I got home after school, Daddy had installed a new front door. The living room was back the way it used to be, Liz was gone, and my mother didn't speak to my grandmother for a week.

Then she was sick, lying in bed twenty-four hours a day, day after day. She cried and whimpered. My grandmother took her in to see the doctor and he put her in the hospital again, this time at Wichita General, where they did the hysterectomy they should have done before. She came home looking tired and went to bed for two months. Her eyebrows and eyelashes fell out, a reaction to the anesthetic. Besides the difficult recuperation from major surgery, she had other problems. Her skin took on a peculiar yellow cast; she had contracted hepatitis in the hospital. It seemed crazy, but she had to go back to the hospital to get well from what she had caught there. When she came home again, she lay on her bed facing away from the door, living on tea, applesauce, poached eggs, and toast. She was thin with a little potbelly. I tried to tell her about school, but I could see she didn't care. After a few weeks, I got used to a new routine. After school I sat with her, even if she was asleep, but I didn't try to talk. Sometimes I read a library book, looking up each time I turned a page. Sometimes I pulled a chair alongside her bed and said the Rosary silently, though I held the beads up where she could see them if she looked my way. One day I went in and found her picking at herself with a double-edged razor, pick, pick, pick, little flecks of blood like dots from a fountain pen all along her cuticles and up and down the inside of her wrist. The blood didn't flow. I had never seen such a thing and I don't remember being frightened so much as curious, but I pretended not to notice. I never emulated her cutting, but it wouldn't be many years before I would begin furiously scratching and digging at the pads of my feet to the point of bleeding and infection, something I have done in times of great stress for fifty years.

My grandmother, whose job was hard labor, lost so much weight she had to take in her work pants. Karen just about lived with Ruth. Father Knopf came when he could. The doctor gave Mother shots, then talked to my grandmother in her bedroom with the door shut. Another day Father Daly came out at the same time as the doctor, and they talked with Daddy and my grandmother, all of them standing in the backyard. Crouching, I watched them through the screen door. My grandmother clutched her trousers with one hand and her hair with the other. It looked as if she might pull one off and the other out. One day soon after, I came home from school and Mother was gone. My grandmother said Daddy and Father Knopf had taken her to Dallas where she would get some rest. Rest was all she did, I thought. My grandmother's face was bloated from crying. Daddy didn't come home for several days. Then he got work in Colorado, don't ask me how, and was gone for most of the summer.

Poor Mother. Confined, against her will. When I was her age, twenty-five, I was in Ithaca, New York, in a repertory theater company. Some kind of fellowship was paying me enough to live on with money left over. I was learning mime and juggling, and rehearsing a British accent, dropping acid, and writing poetry about thwarted love.

At twenty-five, my mother has had croup, measles, mumps, chicken pox, ringworm, scarlet fever, two children, two miscarriages, serious kidney infections, anemia, recurrent flu, an entangling fibroid tumor, and a hysterectomy, then the hepatitis. In the Dallas institution she will sit for hours in cold baths and hot baths and she will go to occupational therapy. She will be given shock treatments and come home with an ulcer and an allergy to cow's milk, and when Liz calls her, she will say, *Who? Who?* I know none of these things then, of course. I think of her as away visiting. I don't want to worry, though I begin biting my nails, another lifelong habit. I say my prayers earnestly in case she is too tired to pray where she is.

THE GOOD THING WAS, it was soon summer, and Aunt Mae was in town. She had been married, living in Florida, and had a daughter, Joan Cheryl, almost exactly Karen's age. They would become as close as sisters. She had divorced, returned to Texas, married Howard Perkins, moved with him to West Texas, and had a son, Michael, who was almost two. Howard's parents lived in Wichita Falls, not very far from my grandmother's house, but in a nicer neighborhood. During the summer Mae stayed there for weeks with her kids, and Howard's sisters and their children were in and out, too. Mae took Karen and me along as if we were hers; we would spend most of every summer with her from then on. We even called Howard's mother Granny Perkins. It was great for Karen, who was the right age for the group. I was a little older, but it was fun to play or read under the big trees in the Perkins yard. Mr. Perkins kept the most perfect lawn I've ever seen, with grass as green and soft as a golf course. And when Mae went back to her home in Midland, she took us with her. (They lived someplace different every year or two as Howard made his way up the ladder at Halliburton, the company where he worked.) So though my concerns for my mother were persistent, they were like a background hum behind the clamor of summer, and only at night did I curl into a ball around my cramping stomach and pray for her to come home soon.

I returned in August and found that Mother was home at last, slopping around in a gown and her old mules. Her hair was caught in pigtails or pinned behind her ears. She rouged her lips with old sticks and didn't draw on eyebrows. She gave me a small red wallet that she had made in the hospital from two flat pieces of soft leather. All around the edges, she had punched holes and then stitched the pieces together. I liked the simple wallet for its own sake and because she had made it. I carried it around with a nickel and a dime inside until the day she snapped at me, saying she couldn't stand to look at it anymore.

Much later I wondered about the months she was gone. I must have asked her what she had been sick with, and what they did for her. She had cooled off by then, and she assured me that it was a place you went to rest and get strong. "Look at you, you've grown a foot," she said, to distract me. Another time she told me she went there because of her terrible headaches.

I'm sure she said that about the headaches to keep from saying anything about the truth of what kind of place it was, but later on, when I began to have serious migraines, too, I wondered what that would mean to me; for many years I feared I would be put away and have things done to me. I didn't know what those things might be until I read the early feminist critiques of psychiatric treatments for women, and also information about 1950s psychiatric practices in general. Then the hints and tidbits of information she leaked to me over the years added up to a kind of horror story that broke my heart and terrified me.

I don't think Mother ever forgave her mother and her husband for agreeing to put her in a psychiatric hospital. (Such a facility was commonly called a "mental ward.") My grandmother talked with me about it, reluctantly, not long before she died. She said that they had all been afraid she would kill herself. All that crying. The most benign prediction was that she would "waste away." Both Father Knopf and Father Daly had told her and my father that hospitalization was the best thing, the only thing, and they had worked to arrange for diocesan support for most of the expenses. The priests said that in Dallas (where no one in the family could get down to visit her) she would have the sacraments and the diligent attention, not just of doctors, but of priests. She would come home much better. My grandmother would never have done anything she thought would harm Edith. Committing someone to a psychiatric hospital is a desperate, last measure, now as much as then. It was wrenching to yield her child to strangers, but nobody knew what to do with Edith and they all had work to do. Depression never has been an easy state to grasp or keep patience with.

Mother came home cowed and bitter. For a while, she didn't even seem interested in her faith. A visiting Benedictine priest came by now and then, someone she had met in Subiaco, but

Father Daly said he wanted her to come to the church and the rec-tory—he wanted her to get out of the house—and she didn't seem to have the energy to go so far across town. She rallied to help make Karen's First Communion as special as my own, insisting that she have a new dress and not mine handed down, but I'm cer-tain they never talked about Jesus' body.

Karen was a literal-minded child, with a suspicious air. She lurked on the sidelines with the sly watchfulness of a future spy. She made no demands and never cried. She played with the neigh-bor kids and at night she put herself to bed. She got her first pair of glasses (she had been squinting and rubbing her eyes, and *Mother was paying attention!*). Everyone made a fuss about how cute she was, but I can see in her photographs that the glasses gave her another shield, a way to keep her distance. Whatever were her judgments, she kept them to herself. She didn't live the same childhood that I did, I'm certain of that. A few times, in anger, she has given me a glimpse of her memories and made me feel that she didn't live a childhood at all.

WHAT FINALLY GOT MOTHER out of the house was Ralph Yarborough's 1952 campaign for governor, his first of three unsuc-cessful tries. She had a good spurt of better health, gained weight, and cut her hair. She left the house briskly with an air of urgency. She poured herself into canvassing, mailings, and phone banks. No one cared that she had no high-school diploma and little work experience. She was attractive, bright, committed. She had good instincts—like the time she was supposed to meet Yarborough's plane, but Karen had come down with the mumps. She wrapped a big white dishtowel around Karen's face and took her along; Karen's photograph was on the front page of the newspaper the next day, the little girl who couldn't stay away from the gubernatorial candidate.

Mother really believed in Yarborough, who was called by some "the patron saint of Texas liberals," as she also believed in the intellectual presidential candidate, Adlai Stevenson.

She became more and more important to the campaign. Even at home, the phone was always ringing, and she'd call out, "I'll get it!" We were on a party line, and sometimes I'd hear her say crossly to an impatient neighbor, "I'll be a few more minutes, this is very important. This is about your next governor!" She had high color in her cheeks. My grandmother gave her money to buy two dresses suitable for the office. My favorite was a blue with narrow white stripes that she accessorized with white plastic earrings, short white gloves, and a flat-brimmed straw hat. She was selected to attend the state Democratic convention, and then was selected for the national, but her doctor absolutely forbade her attendance at the latter, and she tearfully gave in.

Unfortunately Yarborough lost the primary to the incumbent governor, R. Allan Shivers. Mother threw herself into Yarborough's 1954 campaign, too, becoming his office manager, but he lost again, accused of accepting the backing of Communist labor unions. (When Yarborough won a vacated senatorial seat and then voted for the Civil Rights Act of 1957, Mother pointed out to me that it was a historic act, but she was by then beyond politics, lost in the pain of her debilitating illness.)

Mother got part-time work in the office of a lawyer she had met during the campaign. Daddy began to get steadier work, too. At night she made monkey dolls out of men's socks, a mountain of them, to raise money for our Christmas presents. I sewed on the button eyes. In December I went door to door after school and on Saturdays, carrying her big straw purse stuffed with dolls. They had black button eyes, red embroidered mouths, and long skinny limbs that hung over the edge of the purse. They were like little orphans needing a home. I had no trouble at all selling them. I was proud, going home with a stack of dollar bills and turning them over to my mother. Life settled into routine.

I took an early city bus and attended Mass every morning before school, and Mother took Karen and me to Mass on Sundays. Early in 1953 we were able to move to a place of our own in a city housing project. By then I desperately wanted to win Mother back to our old intimacy, which I equated with devotion to the Rosary. Her pretty blond hair was fading and dry, and I was afraid she was getting sick again. The bloating of her stomach no longer went down, and she was too unsteady on her feet to wear heels, but her health improved in our new place, and pray and study and play we did. She found a retired English teacher to tutor me in writing poetry (meter, rhyme). There was a contest sponsored by Midwestern University's music department, to give low-income children opportunities with classical instruments. AMI had already offered me free piano lessons, beginning in sixth grade, so Mother took Karen to the Midwestern program, which gave her a free violin and private lessons twice a month. Karen's photograph was in the newspaper again, and I keenly envied that, wanting to do something special enough to make the paper, too. Then I reminded myself that what Mother and I had, and did, was more special than politics or music. Like the time we made our own paper dolls and drew nuns' habits for them, dark brown like the Carmelites'. She showed me how a young novice might have to lie flat on the floor in front of the superior and confess her faults: *I broke silence. I ate extra dessert.* Caught up in the spirit of our play, she suggested that "all of us" say the Rosary, and we propped up the congregation of paper nuns on the altar while we prayed.

My mother needed God to keep her well, and I thought she needed me, too. This belief was the bedrock of my relationship with her. Right up until the day she died, I thought I could rally the heavenly troops and keep her going.

I had no inkling of our move to our own place until a few days before it happened. I begged not to go. I didn't think my grandmother's house was crowded. I didn't remember Ohio. I was nine years old and all I remembered was living with her. I even called her "Mommy." All the grandkids took after me and did the same.

Daddy was working for a construction company, learning carpentry skills, and he and Mother were able to save the required small deposit and buy a few pieces of cheap furniture. We were going to a duplex in a housing development for low-income families. It was across a dirt road and railroad tracks, far from my grandmother's neighborhood. Our building was made of pale green cinder blocks, and the rough inner walls were easy purchase for silverfish. Karen and I slept together in a bed that we kept pulled out a foot from the wall.

We were at one end of a long string of apartments. It helped the transition that the new place had a rural feel like the area around my grandmother's North Lamar Street house, mostly because its streets, wide and little used, were unpaved. My parents bought me a bicycle and after some false starts and a lot of tears, I learned to ride it. Mother liked having neighbors of her own, people her mother didn't know, and of course Daddy was relieved to be out of Frieda's house. Once he said, heck, if we were going to live in barracks, he should have stayed in the Air Force. That was how I pieced together the way my parents had met. He had been at Sheppard Air Force Base during the war, which ended before he got shipped out. Mother had been working in a café and once he had seen her there, he went back again and again. I eventually asked my grandmother about it. She told me a little story that I later heard again from my aunt. Dean ("R. D." Hupp) had been invited to supper and my grandmother served a heaping platter of fried chicken. The chicken was fresh from her mother's farm. Although he was offered first choice, he took a back, a neck, and a wing. *Thank you, Mrs. Hambleton*, he said. *Looks real good.* Obviously, my grandmother said, he was impossibly Yankee, raised to be stingy even with himself. She made him sound lumbering and stupid, though Mother had liked him well enough to marry him. She sneered, *He didn't even finish training*, referring to his stint at the base, though the end of the war was hardly his doing. *She thought he was a ticket out of town*, my grandmother said. Which he was. The surprise, I think, for both him and Mother, was that they ended up back in Frieda's house. I liked to think that it had to do with Mother's longing for her mother, and was not the result of some failure on Daddy's part, but I knew it was complicated and a cause for shame and resentment. Little bits of conversation began to make sense to me: *He left Ohio in the nick of time.* The subtext was that he would have been caught at something, but what? I think my grandmother would have told me more if I had asked, but I didn't want to hear something bad about him, and when I was grown, I didn't want to hear about him at all.

A nice family lived on the other side of our duplex. They were Mexicans who had moved up from Del Rio. There were other Mexicans in the project, but they didn't speak much English and Mother didn't get to know them, and because she was always seen with Elpidia, the next-door neighbor, the white women in the project snubbed her. Mother didn't care. She and Elpidia became fast friends and went to the store together and to church together for novenas or weekday Mass, hauling Elpidia's babies along. When Mother didn't feel well, she could send Karen over to play with the babies. I was too old to need baby-sitting, but I was considered too young to look after my sister. I spent my free time with books and paper dolls; I thought of myself as my mother's companion. There was no one for me to play with, though I did not mind. I could always read.

The arrangement didn't please my grandmother. Uncle Howard, who worked for Halliburton, had been trying to get Daddy a job. Uncle Howard said that Daddy just needed to drive to Dallas and take a few tests, prove he was literate, and he would be a shoo-in. But I guess Daddy wanted to get a job on his own, even if it wasn't a very good one.

The day we moved to the duplex, my grandmother said it was throwing money away to go and live in a project for Mexicans, when she was going to be moving into a brand-new house with two bedrooms and cots and a new couch that let down. Daddy went in and out of her house that day, carrying boxes of our belongings to the car, brushing by her on the steps without looking at her or saying anything. He never quarreled with my grandmother, but he sometimes took on an aggravating stolidity that brought fury to her face. I felt sorry for him and sorry for her. I never understood the power of passivity until I encountered it in a lover; even good men go to silence by default, and more times than not get their way. Much later I would send letters into my father's silence, and I would understand better how it felt to be on the receiving end.

My grandmother stood in the doorway and watched, her arms rigid at her sides, until my mother sent me and my sister to sit in the car. Daddy came out. "Guess that's it," he said, and went straight to the car and got in without looking at her. I heard Mother say, "It's my life, Mother!" When she slammed the car door it was like a gunshot.

My grandmother jumped onto the running board of our old coupe, on my father's side, and grabbed his shoulder through the open window. "What have you got to be so proud about?" she yelled. "When have you had a better job than Howard can get you? When have you ever been the one to feed your kids?" Daddy started the car and backed up slowly while my grandmother hung on, screaming. By then Karen was squalling and I was shrieking, "Mommy! Mommy!" with my arms outstretched, while my mother slapped at me to keep quiet and my grandmother yelled, "Those children should have better!" and hit my father's shoulder until he reached across the steering wheel with his right hand and shoved her hard away.

It was months before Mother let my grandmother come to our

house. I was allowed to talk to her on the telephone, and I told her about my swimming lessons at the Boys Club, how cold and delicious it was to come out into the night afterward and jump into the warm car where Mother or Daddy waited for me. I told her about school, and my poetry writing lessons. She always said, "That's good, precious," no matter what I said.

At Christmas she came by with sacks of groceries and presents for Karen and me, and we gave her small gifts we had purchased at the dime store. I had written a poem (my own) on the back of a postcard that had pictures of roses, her favorite flower. The last line said, "I put my fingers on my cheeks to find the places where you kissed me." She didn't look at it then; I knew that later she would read it. She would wonder if I would grow up and learn to be angry with her like Mother. I know because she used to tell me she expected it, and I would argue fiercely that I would love her always, and I would cling to her until she said she knew I would. She didn't stay long. I followed her outside and hugged her, then went in and cried myself to sleep. We began to see her again after that, sometimes at our house, and sometimes at a park if it wasn't too cold, or at a café. She had moved into the new house on Grant Street in a new part of town. It wasn't much larger than the first house, but of course it was new, and it was a lot closer to the mill. She told me she had planted apricot and pecan trees in the back, and in the front, rosebushes that came from Oregon. In the spring she planted tomatoes, okra, onions, and squash. That's the house I think of when I think of home, the house I lived in after college, the house where I went to see her until she died in 1983.

It was a long time before we visited the new house, although we drove by it once. Mother wouldn't let me go to spend the night. My grandmother had begun seeing a man who worked at the feed mill on the same road where General Mills was, and Mother didn't want us to be around him. She didn't say why. After some months, my grandmother married the man, whom she called by his last name, Hammond. Eventually I did go to the house when he was there a few times. I was nervous around him. He was a gruff man and uneasy with me in the room. He had a daughter who spent one weekend a month with him. She was my age, a polite, smart girl. Hammond yelled at her and sometimes hit her, swinging his arm and knocking her shoulder or even the side of her head. Once he yanked her out into the backyard and beat her with a belt while my grandmother and I stood under the door frame into her bedroom like people in a tornado. I heard Mother talking to Daddy about Hammond. Daddy said, "It's hard to figure, ain't it?" I guess nobody stopped to think that Frieda wasn't fifty years old yet, that she might have womanly feelings left, might be lonely after nearly twenty years widowed.

One thing that happened in the project upset my mother terribly. Two Saturdays before Christmas, some people from a Baptist youth group came to our door. Karen and I were still in pajamas, eating cereal. Mother opened the door and these kids started singing a carol and then one of them held out a box of food. I could see the red ribbon around a canned ham. She was just beside herself. The kid explained that the youth fellowship had raised money for the food boxes, but Mother cut her off and said she didn't need Baptist charity, and slammed the door. Then she sat on our ugly shiny vinyl couch and cried until she was hiccuping. Karen and I sat on each side of her, patting her arms and saying, "That was awful, Mama, that was just awful." We didn't have any idea what had happened, really, and of course it was never again mentioned.

·

THAT SUMMER OUR MOTHER drove us girls across the Red
River into Oklahoma to the farm for Sunday dinner a couple of
times, and everyone was civil. I don't remember Daddy ever going.
The farm belonged to my grandmother's mother and stepfather,
and nobody would have made a scene in front of them. They were
as far back as the living family went, and their age and labor and
decency gave them unassailable dignity.

One Sunday Mother wasn't feeling well so she lay on my great-
grandmother's bed most of the afternoon, her face turned to the
inside wall toward a paper field of buttercups on cream browned
by age like something baking. She had been weeping for the
Rosenbergs. She had explained to me about their execution (a few
days before Mother's birthday, spoiling it), and that it was a terrible mistake. I could not believe in the possibility of execution, or
perhaps it was only that I could not believe it could be a mistake.
I worried that my mother was sick because she misunderstood, or
vice versa. I asked my grandmother about the Rosenbergs, and she
snapped, "That's what we have a government for, to worry about
such things!"

The big worry was my mother. My grandmother sent me into
the bedroom with a cool drink and a basin of ice water. I dipped a
washcloth into the cold water, wrung it out, and gave it to my
mother to lay across her forehead. Eventually she got up and ate
some leftover dumplings and sat in the kitchen with the other
women—my grandmother, her sister and a sister-in-law, and my
great-grandmother. They were stringing green beans and mending,
never just sitting. Mother said casually that we were going to take

a trip in late July to see Daddy's family in Ohio. My grandmother looked so startled my mother said, "We are coming back, you know." My grandmother asked if she could come over to tell us goodbye. They set a time as if it were a dental appointment. The other women pretended not to be listening.

On the evening my grandmother was coming, Mother made us get dressed in the cowboy outfits she and Daddy had bought us for the trip: fringed leather jackets, boots, blue jeans, and cowboy hats. Mother had worked for three months as a waitress in an Italian restaurant to get the money for the trip, and the evening my grandmother came by, Mother was dressed in a short, tight black skirt and a blouse with a scooped neck. She wore dark red lipstick and extravagantly penciled eyebrows. She told my grandmother that she got better tips if she looked a little glamorous.

The whole time my grandmother was there, neither of them sat down and Daddy stayed in the bedroom down the hall, listening to *People Are Funny* on the radio. We heard him blow his nose a couple of times.

I went outside with my grandmother and we talked about the trip as we stood by her car. On the way to Ohio, Mother was taking us to visit the monastery in Arkansas where she had once gone on retreat, and we planned to spend the night there. My grandmother wasn't impressed. She was waiting for me to get done talking so she could give me advice. She said, "Now don't you worry too much if those Hupps are a cold bunch. They might not like you because you're the *older* child." That didn't make any sense to me but I didn't say anything. She reminded me that I could call her collect. She had me pretend that she was the operator, to show her that I knew how to make the call.

"And one more thing, precious," she said. She took something out of the glove compartment of her car, a little purse. "This is a little money, for emergencies. It's a trust. Do you understand?"

"Trust? Believing something?"

"It means you hold onto it and you don't lose it or talk about it." I didn't know what to say. "If nothing goes wrong," she went on, "you come back and nobody needs to know you ever had it." She looked determined. "Your mother has planned this trip against the bone, as if things don't go wrong." She put the purse in my hand. "This way they won't have to call and ask me. They won't have to wait for it to come. And I won't worry, because I'll know you have it."

"I'll be careful," I said. It was thrilling. I kissed her and went back into the house.

When we heard her car drive away, Daddy came into the living room in his boxer shorts and sat on the couch to cut his toenails. Mother looked at him disgustedly, grabbed her sweater, and said, "I'm leaving!" without kissing me goodbye.

ONE OF MOTHER'S priest friends had given her a bisque-fired statue of the Blessed Virgin in a kit with delicate brushes, and together we painted it the weekend before the trip to Ohio. Daddy said, "That could wait," but Mother and I didn't bother to argue. We wanted to come home to our altar and the new statue. We wanted to know that it was there waiting for us while we were away. We didn't know what kind of churches we would visit on our trip, or how much we might miss home.

I painted the robes a pale blue with a darker mantle, and she did the face and the hands, except that she allowed me the privilege of painting the tiny rosebud lips. We starched a crocheted doily and laid it on the altar, then set the statue down between two votive candles in milky holders. I asked her if we would take our rosaries to Ohio. She took a moment to think about it and then she said no, she thought not, so we laid them by the candles. We would just say our Hail Marys, counting them on our fingers. "What if we laid them down and left them there, in that awful house?" She said that if any of the Hupps asked me what I was going to be when I grew up, I should say that I didn't know, because they would not understand about vocations, they might even laugh at us. My eyes were round with apprehension; she clasped my hand and said that we would stick close together, she and I.

"What about Karen?" I asked.

She laughed. "Oh, Karen will be fine, you wait and see. She's the baby, see. She's Dean's little baby. They won't let her out of their sight."

It was like what my grandmother had said, that the Hupps preferred little kids. The thought that Karen might be the center of attention was curious to me, but I did not mind. Why would I want the attention of Yankee strangers? I would stick close to Mother, as she had said. I would pray in secret, like a Roman girl in pagan times.

EVERYTHING ABOUT THE TRIP to Ohio was an adventure, from Burma Shave signs to overnights in rooming houses. We saw a two-headed calf, and visited some caverns. In a park in Arkansas, I watched my mother lie with her head in Daddy's lap while he drank beer from a cold brown bottle. At the Subiaco Abbey, we saw the big presses where the brothers made Communion wafers, and we sat behind wooden grilles in the chapel and heard the brothers chant plainsong. In St. Louis, we stayed in a hotel, and I had my first migraine headache. Mother sent Daddy and Karen off to their supper and stayed behind to take care of me. She wet a washrag in cold water and laid it across my eyes. She said "Shhh," and "Big girl," until I fell asleep. I started to tell her about the money my grandmother had given me, but I couldn't find the words. I thought about it in the car the next morning, how even if my headache was like hers, it was my own pain, how if I kept the money secret and Mother's plans worked out, I'd tell my grandmother we never needed her money, and I'd never take a trust like that again.

BECAUSE DADDY'S PARENTS LIVED on a farm in Ohio, I thought I knew what to expect. I was used to summer Sundays at my great-grandparents' farm, where puffs of red dust lined my nose, and I ran barefoot until I burned flat wet blisters on the balls of my feet. But this was another country. Rolling hills filled the horizon, and the houses had basements. In my grandparents' house a staircase curved down to a banister with a beveled post; the steps were carpeted. Outside, rows of apple trees stood in lines like soldiers behind the house, and to the side, a neighbor's field of barley was going from green to gold. My grandmother raised vegetables in a plot the size of a double bed. Grandfather Hupp, not a farmer but a railroad clerk, had his own horizon.

One afternoon he took me on his little tractor. Down a corridor in the trees we went, toward the place at the end where they seemed to come together and then widen as you approached. I thought of Mother's drawing lessons with me when I was a little girl. I tried to tell him how different this was from my great-grandparents' Oklahoma farm, with its wobbling vistas of yellow wheat and red dirt. He shook his head. He didn't understand why a person would want that. He didn't understand why his son stayed in Texas, which he called "the South." Later, I reminded myself over and over that Grandfather took me, and me alone, on that jaunt through the orchard; that he did like me and not just Karen, even if no other Hupps liked me at all.

More remarkable than the land was the way Daddy was special in his family. His teenage sister, Patty, followed him around, and he tinkered with her bike. His mother heaped his plates so full the food oozed over the edge. She inspected his collars, and a day later, new shirts appeared on his bed. She boiled his undershirts in a pot with bluing. She never looked my mother in the eye.

Daddy found chores to do for his mother or went into town with his father. Karen regressed. No longer six years old, capable of changing the neighbor baby's diaper, capable of scrambling her own egg and making her bed, she followed our grandmother around all day, speaking in a baby's voice. Mother and I were on our own. Downstairs by the big boiler we found piles of magazines on a daybed, and the musty basement became our hideaway. No one looked for us there or anywhere. Sometimes the rest of them went on little outings without asking us along. I asked my mother why they did that and she shrugged, unperturbed. *She* didn't like *them,* either. I didn't really have an opinion; they were strangers. If they didn't like my mother, I didn't really want them to like me. *Yeah, who cares?* I said, and Mother, looking at me over the pages of her magazine, blew me a kiss.

I had never heard Daddy talk so much. He and his father talked about the economy and the orchards, about baseball, and about people whose names I didn't know. His mother sat with her back straight, looking like someone made of hardwood, her hair wound in braids that strained her hairline.

Grandfather said he thought we should have blown North Korea to hell and back. He thought the commies would end up on his front steps. Mother bit her lip and refused dessert. Grandfather finally ran down and there was only the sound of cutlery on china, Daddy chewing, and sometimes Karen's chatter. Patty leaned over and gave her choice morsels of food. Pale-haired, chubby, bespectacled, and newly confident, my sister did no wrong.

DADDY'S OLDER SISTER, ROSEANNE, lived in a suburb of Washington, D.C., with her husband, a state trooper, and their three boys. We went to see them, traveling in the Hupps' big Buick. Karen rode in front between the men. I rode in back between the women, who never spoke. When we stopped for the night at a spindly house that said "*ROOMS*," Mother said she was too tired to eat and I stayed behind with her, though I was hungry. After the coast was clear, we went downstairs and up the street to a corner grocery and bought chocolate bars.

Back in the room we gobbled our candy and drank water from the spigot, laughing in happy conspiracy and escape. She combed my hair and plaited it, and then I begged to do hers.

I was gentle as I could be, seeing how thin her hair was at the crown. In the mirror she watched me. She took the brush and scooted over, patting the stool to make a place for me. Side by side we studied ourselves in the mirror. I saw that I was like her but not like her, too. My eyes were dark, my brows heavy, but I was delicate like her.

She brushed a finger along my cheekbones. I turned and put my arms around her neck. She crooned something about sticking together, by now a familiar theme. She looked so tired all the time. I wished I knew how to make it better. I wanted to be her reason for keeping at it, her reason to believe in the future.

How can life go on if you don't think that it's worth living?

I SAT AT A picnic table in Aunt Roseanne's lush green yard, drawing trees. I wanted to show the light speckling through the leaves onto the tabletop but I didn't know how.

Uncle Matt was playing gin rummy with my mother. Their voices slapped like cards on the table.

"I've got you now!"

"Ha!"

"You can't weasel out of it."

"You're no card player, Edith, you've just got a run of luck. I'll win in the end."

My mother laughed. Her face was a bit sunburned and she was enjoying herself. She was wearing wide-legged, cuffed shorts and a halter top she had made by twisting two squares of cloth together. She laid her last cards on the low table and crowed triumphantly. "Hey, hey, big shot!" I was at an angle behind her, and I could watch Uncle Matt's face as he took in her glee. I didn't understand why he was happy.

Uncle Matt had abundant hair on his chest and shoulders and

Mother had explained that he was Italian. He was rude to everyone except my mother. He gathered up the cards and lined them
up with a sharp rap against the tabletop.

"Be a good sport," Mother said.

"I don't remember that we set any stakes."

"So I get to say what they are now, don't I?"

Uncle Matt smiled. "Try me, cheater."

Mother laughed. "I in-sist. I dee-mand." Her voice was false,
not Texan at all. "I command you to bring me a beer." The beer
bottles were in a cooler an arm's reach away from my uncle.

He cocked his chair to the side and grabbed a beer. Very slowly
he reached to the ground on the other side of his chair, looking
straight at my mother all the while, and his hand came down right
on the opener like magic. He held the bottle just above his belly
button and opened it. My mother leaned back in her chair, tilting
it, holding herself steady with her bare feet on the table edge.

Uncle Matt set the bottle down on the table right in front of
him.

"I can't reach that," Mother said.

Uncle Matt put his bare foot up on the table and slowly
nudged the bottle across the table, a little past center, to my mother's side. It was disgusting.

I thought she ought to tell him straight out to hand her the
beer. I thought the way he pushed it over wasn't nice. She bent
down, both elbows on the table, her chin in her hands, and waited.
He got up slowly and came around the table. He picked the beer
up by the top of the neck and dangled it in front of my mother's
face. She pulled it against her cheek. He turned around and when
he did he caught me staring.

"Watch your mommy while I go in the house. Don't let her
stack the deck."

Aunt Roseanne was standing on the step with her arms crossed, leaning against the door. She stepped aside neatly to let him in. "Mind what he says," she said.

ON THE STEPS OF THE moldy basement, I heard my mother's voice, though I couldn't hear what she was saying. Uncle Matt had gone down for more drinks and mother had followed him. Aunt Roseanne called after: "See if there's a bottle of Chablis."

I could see Mother's white throat, her flat breasts above and between the checked straps of her halter top. Uncle Matt ran his hand down the side of her throat and onto her breasts. She sucked air in, raspy and long. I crouched on the upper step in the dark. I saw his hand go around to her bottom while the other hand slid down her front.

I SLEPT ON A SMELLY SOFA in a tiny room piled with books and boxes. In the night I got up to go to the bathroom and almost screamed when a door opened right in front of me and there was Uncle Matt. He took a step to block my way. Sleepy, confused, I stared at him and waited. He grinned and bent closer, as if to study something in my eye. He reached over and tucked a straggly hair behind my ear. My sleeping parents were only a few steps away.

"Gonna look just like your sweet mother," he growled.

"I have to go."

"You're just a little twig off her tree." He put his big hand on my shoulder and moved closer. I could feel the heat from his body. With his index finger he touched me on the exact spot that was the pale promise of my nipple. I knew he touched me, but I didn't really feel it. He leaned closer and cupped my hip, trailing his finger inward.

I reached up with both hands and shoved hard. His fingers dug into my shoulder, into my thigh. I pushed past. In the bathroom I cried with my face in a towel and then went down the empty hall. I moved boxes and chairs against the inside of the closed door and after a long while I slept.

The next day was hot and muggy and after lunch my mother said she had to lie down. She said she was all worn out. Everyone was going to a swimming pool.

"Get your suit, sport," Daddy said.

"It hurts behind my eye."

"Uh-oh," Daddy said.

Everyone left, even Uncle Matt, looking like a bear in his swim trunks.

My mother and I lay on her bed with a fan blowing across us.

I wondered why my mother liked Uncle Matt. I wondered why she couldn't see that he was a bad man. I thought that once I told her about last night, she wouldn't like him anymore.

He stood in front of me just to be mean, I would say. *He wouldn't let me go by.*

He touched me here.

What I said was, "I saw you last night."

I didn't think she was listening.

"In the basement."

She whipped her head around and stared at me with hateful eyes. She had never looked at me like that before.

Then she reached out and stroked my hair, making my skin crawl. "You're just a little little girl."

"I did, I saw you," I said, but she had turned away.

I thought of my grandmother's money in my suitcase.

I thought of my uncle's hands on me.

I wanted to say, *I'm big enough for keeping secrets. I know more than you would guess.* But she wouldn't believe me unless I told her things that surprised her, and then she would know everything.

OUTSIDE OKLAHOMA CITY, half a day from home, the car broke down. We stood around on the side of the road while Daddy poked at things under the hood. He motioned us all to get back in. "We can get to town," he said. "With our fingers crossed."

We parked on the street by a garage. Sweat trickled down my mother's face. Daddy's neck was a deep purplish red.

"I'll call Mother," my mother said.

"Wait," I said, just above a whisper. They turned to stare at me. "I've got some money. Mommy gave it to me. For emergencies."

We took my suitcase out of the trunk of the car. They watched me dig under my clothes and come up with the little snap purse.

Daddy's face was streaked white around his nose and chin. Mother was speechless. I threw the money into the front seat of the car and ran down the street, my face burning.

. . .

School started. Now I was ten. Once again there was the happy routine of daily Mass, the Rosary, the buses back and forth to school, radio programs two or three nights a week. Mother taught me to make spaghetti sauce and vegetable soup.

Daddy got a good job working for a patio contractor. He was learning to make lightweight, pastel-colored bricks. He said there was a big future in it. The other helper was a Negro man, and Mother met his wife and liked her. They all talked about Daddy and the Negro man starting their own business one day. Sometimes Mother and I drove to colored town and sat in the woman's kitchen while she ironed clothes, ten cents a piece. The houses on her street were wood and tar paper and sheets of tin, with ramshackle porches and dirt yards. The women talked about their kids and about recipes, about politics (I didn't follow much of it) and the weather. Mother enjoyed the visits. The woman never came to our house.

Daddy was doing so well we didn't need to stay in public housing. We moved to a house on a bluff just above the high-school football stadium. The first game night after we moved in, a man came to our door and said he'd pay a dollar to park in our driveway. After that, on game nights, I was out with a flashlight, taking money. I was able to fit four cars in the long drive that went from the street past the side of our house to the alley. I bought Mother a teacup and saucer at the drugstore that I passed every day on the way to school; the clerk said it was bone china.

The house was nice. It had two bedrooms, a kitchen and dining room, living room, and a room at the back that we called the den. Besides that, there was a little porch where we put an old school desk Mother found at a junk shop, and I sat out there in nice weather to draw and write my poems and stories. I wrote about a painter who was blinded and who fell in love with a singer who lost her voice. I wrote about orphans making their way through the woods toward a distant village where no children had ever been born. I wrote poems about saints and Mother sent them in to the diocesan newsletter and they were published. I started writing a novel about a girl who had a vision no one believed. I can't remember what it was she saw, but I know why I abandoned it. I couldn't make things come out balanced, as I had in the stories. I was mad for solving problems.

We had a big, fenced backyard, and Mother said it was perfect for baby-sitting. She put an ad in the paper and in no time we had four little kids spending the day right up to supper time. Mother got a little part-Scottie dog we named Blackie, from the pound. She was feeling well again, and I think we were all happy. There were lots of children in the neighborhood, and we all played up and down the street, in backyards and fronts. Nobody seemed to mind our running around in their yards. Once or twice a week Mr. Oechsner, an electrician, drove his pickup slowly up and down the block after supper, honking. Whatever kids were around piled in the back and Mr. Oechsner drove us down to the cemetery and slowly through the grave sites. Afterward, in hot weather, he bought us Popsicles. While we ate, he told us a story about some of the dead, always making them sound like nice people. He warned us to watch for speeding cars, black widow spiders, and rusty nails.

Mother and I put the altar up in the dining room. She borrowed books from the rectory's library for me to read about the saints on my own. I drew illustrations of their martyrdoms and we hung them on the walls of the porch above my desk. She bought Daddy a harmonica, and he sat on the back step and tried to learn to play it. He bought a couple of used tennis rackets and took Karen and me to the park to hit balls back and forth. We went to movies at the drive-in, a family outing we all loved.

Then Daddy's boss fired the Negro laborer. Daddy took up for his friend and so the boss fired him, too. The two couples got together at our house for the first time-—neighbors saw them coming up our walk and later asked Mother who they were-—and the two men thought they could make a go of it on their own. They had good skills now, experience, and they knew a lot of people. Both of them had a little savings. Daddy put a sign up on our lawn: HUPP & TUCKER CONTRACTING. I asked him if people would see it and come to our house to get things built, and he laughed and rubbed the top of my head with his knuckle.

The thing was, the people he had worked for were well-known in town. They had a lot of power, and nobody thought Hupp and Tucker ought to be in business together. Mr. Tucker could have worked for Daddy, maybe, and they would have been all right. But as it was, nobody would extend them credit, and though they did a few small jobs like new porches and some painting, they couldn't make a go of it. I remember Mr. Oechsner coming to the house, talking quietly with Daddy on the porch, and their shaking hands before he left. He had come to say how sorry he was and Daddy had asked him if he had any work, but you had to have training for what an electrician did.

Daddy went back to day labor and he started selling Watkins products door-to-door, but he was having a hard time making the rent. If it hadn't been for Mother's baby-sitting, we would have had to move back in with my grandmother. I didn't want to, a surprise. I liked all of us in the house on Sixth Street. I liked the block, too. My grandmother's ornery husband had been killed in a drunk-driving accident (no one else was hurt), so she might have been glad for the company, but we kept going, a month at a time, on our own.

Daddy talked to Uncle Howard about getting on with

Halliburton. Howard made an appointment for him in Dallas, where he would have to take some tests and interviews. Mother got up in the dark to press his clothes so he would look sharp.

When Daddy finally arrived in Dallas, though, he got off the elevator on the wrong floor and ended up applying for a job with an entirely different company, Otis Engineering. He would never work for anyone else. At first he balked at the hours and the conditions, but Howard told him that in the oil fields he could make himself valuable through sheer doggedness. It was grunt work and you had to be hungry enough for it, but if you could be depended on and you had half a brain, things would get better. Daddy saw guys dropping off on just about any given day and he could see that if he kept showing up, eventually he would be telling the new ones what to do. So if he got a cold, he packed onion-and-butter sandwiches and went out anyway. If he didn't have time to drive home to bed, he slept in the cab of a truck. If somebody else avoided nasty or dangerous work, he took it on. What he hated most was cold weather; he loved to tell us how there was a snowstorm on his very first day. My aunt sniffs: *He thought that made him a hero.* Once he had an opportunity to join Red Adair and Boots Hansen in Houston in their famous business, Boots & Coots Well Control, fighting oil-well hellfires and blowouts, but he stuck with Otis, out of loyalty or timidity. He didn't get rich, but he steadily inched his way up, promotion by promotion. Many years later, the company would be acquired by Halliburton. By then Daddy would have a better job than Howard ever did and my mother would be dead and I would live in another part of the country like one disappeared from my childhood and my father's memory entirely. He lived a long time in Saudi Arabia with his second wife and became the company's regional bigwig. He did fine and still does for all I know, with Uncle Howard and Frieda both in the ground. He didn't just last with Otis, he lived to have a real retirement, an accomplishment in my family that rivaled graduating from college. I wonder if the rest of us ever cross his mind, if he ever thinks, *I guess I showed them.*

HE MOVED OUT TO ODESSA alone so that he could save enough money for the rest of us to move later. He found a room to rent in a house owned by the widow of an oilman. We went to see him there one weekend and she fussed over Karen and me and then I saw that she fussed over Daddy. Mother saw it too. She said, *Isn't it nice she makes it so comfortable for you?* and I could tell she meant something else.

Early one May Saturday, we had a tornado in Wichita Falls. We were just sitting down to soup and crackers when the siren shrilled. It went on and on, so we knew it was not a practice run. Mother and Karen and I and our little dog Blackie crawled under a mattress pulled from the bed onto the floor out in the den. From where I lay, I could see boxes of Watkins vanilla left behind when Daddy jumped ship for Otis. The three of us said the Rosary and complained about the heat. The mattress was too heavy on our backs. Mother dragged a couple of chairs out and propped one end of the mattress up to make a tiny tent. The funnel went overhead and the racket seemed like the end of the world. Karen and I clung to Mother, crying, and the dog ran back and forth from the front door to us, sliding on her rear and making us laugh. We stayed under the mattress until the all-clear rang. We went outside with all the neighbors and saw that below us the tornado had hit the bluff and had torn off part of the stadium. Then we went back inside and reheated our soup.

When Monday came, I refused to go back to school. I wouldn't leave my mother. She begged and tried scolding me, but I cried and clung to her and wouldn't eat. When she said I didn't have any choice, I went into her medicine cabinet and took a lot of what was in there and then threw it all back up. Calmly, she took care of me, then slept in my bed with me that night.

So Karen went by herself to school, walking alone over a mile, hesitant but resigned. I missed the May Day procession when Mary's statue was crowned with a circle of flowers. I missed the strewing of rose petals from the school yard to the church steps. I missed achievement tests and our class party, and the worst thing was, I couldn't find the class minutes.

I was the class secretary. My teacher called to say the class needed to know where the minutes were before they had the last meeting of the year. I have not the vaguest memory of what kind of business a sixth-grade class would have, but I remember well that they could not find them in my desk or in the classroom, and we could not find them at home. I became completely hysterical, and I wasn't one bit better until Mother told the school that I wasn't going to come back at all. Completely frustrated, she fed me with a spoon like a baby, then put me alone on the bus to Midland, where Aunt Mae and Uncle Howard were again living. I perked right up. I learned to make meat loaf and Red Velvet cake. I read a pile of Readers Digest condensed books. Aunt Mae bought me a little watercolor kit. After a while, Karen came out, too. (Mother was working for the second Yarborough senatorial campaign.) In July, Karen and I went to a Baptist tent revival with Aunt Mae, saw a baptism, and sang at the top of our lungs. In the fifties, ecumenism was a sin for Catholics, but when I brought it up, Aunt Mae pointed out that it is polite, when you are a guest, to do what your hostess does, and hadn't we had fun? Under the covers, I said dozens of extra Hail Marys and convinced myself that Aunt Mae was right and that it wasn't like I *believed* anything at the revival. I just liked singing.

Mother spent the summer managing Yarborough's campaign office. In August, when Karen and I went home, one of her priests came to see her. He was another Benedictine she knew from Subiaco. He had come to conduct a retreat. He had a beautiful voice and expressive gestures and his services were popular. He played the clarinet at a church supper in the parish hall. And he called to say he would come to our house.

Mother rushed home early on the day of the visit. She served him pimento-cheese sandwiches with the crusts cut off, and iced tea. Karen was napping and I was out on the porch. After a while she called me in to sit with them in the dining room.

She told him how we had always prayed together and that we had talked about the possibility of a religious vocation for me. Together we had read the journal of the Little Flower, Saint Thérèse of Lisieux, who had received a special papal dispensation to enter the Carmelites at a tender age.

The priest asked me some questions and looked at my drawings. He seemed interested and encouraging, but it was all a trick to make me trust him. When he started saying what he thought of all he had heard, he made me feel small and hateful and exiled in my own home. He dismissed my work as childish. The worst thing was I had been so unguarded.

He admired our altar and asked me how I used it. I said that sometimes at night when I couldn't sleep I came there to kneel and talk to God.

Behind him, my mother smiled.

"And what do you say to God?"

"That I love him. That I wonder what I will become. And I ask him to take care of Mother."

He said that I was too young to speak to God directly. I should limit myself to memorized prayers and perhaps the Rosary with my mother. I should wait until I was mature before I "asserted" myself.

Mother did nothing. She avoided my eyes. She had encouraged my pious behaviors, had made me feel that I had special gifts, a preferred connection, but she said nothing against the priest's condescension. I saw it as a terrible lack of loyalty. It was then, I think, that I began to believe that Mother loved her priests in some forbidden way. Her attachments were too intense, too fraught with neediness. It wasn't proper.

Of course, as soon as the priest was gone, Mother gathered me in her arms and begged me to forgive her. She said she had been too intimidated to contradict him—he was a priest! She said he didn't understand how special I was, he thought I was a *child*. In her embrace, I forgot my resentment.

At Christmas we went to Odessa to visit Daddy and together they rented a house, then Mother and Karen and I returned to Wichita Falls to close up the house on Sixth. The campaign was over (another loss), school was on break, Mother had no income. It didn't make sense to stay in Wichita Falls any longer.

My grandmother wanted us to stay with her until Daddy was on his feet. Mother pointed out that he had been in Odessa working and living alone for months now, and all of us were lonely. We were a family, she pointed out, and we belonged together.

Something about that conversation infuriated Mother, perhaps the unspoken criticism of Daddy that she always sensed in my grandmother's attitude, a criticism that Mother surely interpreted as an insult to her own judgment. Or maybe that time my grandmother just came out and said it: *I hope this job lasts,* the same as saying, *You know damned well it won't.*

·THREE·

The principal, Sister Mary John, and my piano teacher, Sister Francis Joseph, met with my mother when she came to withdraw my sister and me from school. They agreed that Karen was too young to be apart from her mother, but they thought I was capable of settling into convent life for the rest of the academic year, and if it went well, I could return for eighth grade and study for Confirmation with my class. The sisters told Mother that she could continue paying the same modest tuition—there would be no fee for my board—until the family was "on its feet."

The Academy of Mary Immaculate had been central to my life

since my mother's conversion to Catholicism in 1950, and she didn't put up much of an argument against leaving me there, except to say, "I'm afraid I won't know her anymore." It was the most significant decision of my young life, but everyone thought it was for the best, and no one stopped to consider what was being changed, and lost, for the sake of my Catholic education. I don't suppose Daddy was consulted, or would have had anything to say about it, and it was presented to me as a grand surprise: *Wait 'til you hear, honey, what the nuns are going to do for you.*

I couldn't help wondering what public school would be like if I went to Odessa, but the idea of being a *boarder* thrilled me. I thought I would be a puppy nun. I wondered if boarders wore uniform pajamas and recited their night prayers together.

They didn't, though it wouldn't have been much of a stretch. At first, it seemed that heaven had opened a side door and let me in. Convent life was full of secrets and ritual, smells of incense and wax, the creaking of a building already seventy years old. Boarding school took me to higher ground, with its air of orphanhood, the Sunday hailstorms of lonesomeness, the cool spare rituals of an ordered life. The sisters were strict but almost never scolding. I craved their approval, and if some anomalous behavior on my part merited disciplinary attention ("A word with you, dear?" a sister would say), I rushed to defend myself as the guiltless victim of a misunderstanding. Once I went into the chapel for early Mass with the sisters, and I forgot to put on my beret. A crotchety sister tapped me on the shoulder and led me out into the hall, where she sent me away for having improper attire. *It was an accident!* I cried. She shushed me, her bony finger at her lips. *Six o'clock in the morning!* I wept so bitterly, I became nauseated and had to be put to bed with tea and crackers and the mistress's soothing assurances. *Of course it was just a slip,* she said. *So early for such a little girl.* She didn't make me feel much better.

Such incidents were rare, though. I was the perfect student, the good girl. I went to Mass every morning, reciting all the given lines. I went to Rosary many evenings after supper. I try to remember what I was thinking. Was I showing off? There were very old sisters and a few young ones who attended. I think I went for the company and the comfort. The repetition of the familiar words was soothing; after all, I had said them hundreds of times with my mother. When I was alone I couldn't think of anything to say to God. All my welling thoughts were directed to my mother: *I miss you. I love you. Come get me. I'm doing my best.*

When Mother said I could stay, I felt the pang of the coming separation, but there was this great relief: I wouldn't be leaving my grandmother. I assumed I would spend most weekends with her. I was bewildered when the mistress of boarders told me gently that my mother had left explicit instructions that I was not to go to my grandmother's house at all. Sister said kindly that she had talked to my grandmother herself, on the phone, assuring her of my care and their affection for me and their respect for her, even though my mother trumped it with her authority. There was no mention of any quarrel; I knew Sister would not have pried.

When I began to cry, she patted me on the shoulder and left me for a while to work it out alone. I cried myself dry and was left with a wretched migraine. Sister brought an ice pack and said perhaps I could speak to my grandmother on the phone once a week or so. There was a sit-down pay phone in the basement, and if I went down in the evening, I could speak privately.

I saw immediately that I was left afloat between the two people I loved most in the world. *What was Mother mad about now?*

My grandmother said it wasn't for her to say; my mother said she didn't want me going back and forth. In the back of my mind I didn't believe the separation would last. My mother had been mad at my grandmother before, and time had always healed the breach. Neither spoke to me of their issues. I went from mother to grandmother as if I carried two passports.

I tried to think of it as a temporary affliction that I offered up for the souls in purgatory, the way one offered a trip to the dentist. I thought it would surely move one soul closer to heaven.

OUR SEVENTH-GRADE CLASS had a strong sense of unity. We often had projects that brought us together, like gathering food for a charity drive, selling magazine subscriptions to raise money for the school, or decorating the classroom for holiday seasons. In good weather we had softball games after school, and everyone played, good or not. Boys had a lot more freedom, and they headed off at the end of the day in a kind of pack, but girls mostly just went home.

Unfortunately, there wasn't a single boarder in my own age range. There were two little girls who went home on the weekends, me, and half a dozen high-school girls. I saw myself as affiliated with the latter group, but I suspect they did not. The end effect was that I spent time alone, but I don't remember being sorry about it. I read, played the piano, wrote my poems and letters home, and besides, during the week I was in bed at 8:30, and that doesn't leave a lot of time.

During recess, the boys kept to themselves and took their rough stuff to the far end of the playground. The girls fell neatly into two groups. The larger group was rowdy and sometimes a bit mean; they played tag and kickball, often bickered and threw each other out. They punched one another on the arms like boys and whispered words they wouldn't dare to speak aloud. In class they had to be called by name to coax them to answer. They enjoyed burping without covering their mouths. Our teacher would sometimes growl at them, and in a worst case, make them write statements of penance. (*I will not call names. I will not call names.* 100 times.)

As I look back now, I see how benignly reasonable (if sometimes arbitrary) the sisters were, especially when you consider that it was the fifties, and teachers of all sorts had physical as well as educational dominion over their students. My mother had often said we were fortunate, because this order of nuns (Sisters of Saint Mary of Namur, their motherhouse in Belgium) educated its teachers instead of miring them in the nineteenth century. There were a few sourpusses and cranky elders, but for the most part we thought they were funny and gave them our most visible respect, dips of the head or curtsies, even just passing in the hall. When we played nuns, those were the very ones we mimicked.

My group was made up of tender girls who tested one another's conjugations, exchanged compositions and scraps of art. Most recesses, we played convent. We laid out our rooms with twigs and stones, and circumscribed an altar with great care. When we could get hold of a package of Necco candy wafers, we appointed one of us as priest, who then delivered "Communion" to the rest of us. We were a contemplative order, we said; we could not speak. Whole recesses went by without a word. We moved about with the Chinese shuffle of the old nuns, our palms together, our heads bent. There was a young sister assigned to guard our play; she watched us from a small bench under a tree. If I looked up and caught her eye, she smiled. I never thought that she was amused. I thought that she smiled with pleasure, seeing us, like her, with our minds on God.

One of the mild, sunny days of early January, my classmate Mozelle said, trying not to move her mouth, "There's an old lady watching us, over by the fence." Jennie said, "Shhh!" but the spell was broken. Everyone turned to see.

I knew who it was before I saw her. The cyclone fence came to a height just above her belly; she gripped the smooth top bar as I walked toward her. When I saw the look on her face, when I remembered how she loved me, I knew why I hadn't worried too much about my mother's strange proscription. Nothing would keep my grandmother from me.

We hugged and kissed. She patted my cheeks and smoothed my hair. She asked how school was going, and if I needed anything—underwear, snacks, school supplies. I assured her that I was stocked with everything. She shook her head. "I hope your mother is happy," she said. I hugged her again and promised to meet her the next day.

I understood that she would be there at the fence every day she could, and I depended on her to stave off my loneliness for my mother, and for the familiarity that was lacking in convent life. Every Friday she gave me a dollar, bunched up, her hand to mine, as if she were making a bet or a bribe, and when my own hand closed around the wadded bill, I felt connected to her viscerally, as if the bill delivered a tiny electric shock. I didn't tell her that I had trouble spending it. There was nothing to want and no way to get it. I could buy candy (five cents) at recess twice a week, and on Sunday nights we boarders had milkshakes (twenty-five cents) while we watched *The Loretta Young Show* with our mistress of boarders, the principal, and the principal's elderly retarded sister, Genevieve, who slept in a tiny attic room above our dorm.

Cheerily, I reported assignments, test grades, and composition topics. I mentioned what I was reading. (Every Sunday, I wrote this same information to my mother.) Slowly, over a number of visits, I realized that she didn't care what I had to say; I might have been reciting the Offertory in Latin for all that it mattered. I started to talk about simpler matters: We had a toilet overflow and run into the dormitory. We found the tooth of an animal while we were picking up rocks. Poor retarded Genevieve had learned the chorus of a new song, "Beautiful Dreamer," and sang it constantly up in her garret, then banged on the piano in the refectory while we waited for dinner. Standing by the fence, basking in my grandmother's attention, I even dared to ape Genevieve's gruff, tuneless, madcap yowling. And then, suddenly solemn, I clasped my grandmother's hands and said, "I miss you."

A pattern was set for the rest of our lives. Topics didn't matter to us. We breathed the same air; we touched one another hungrily. Our meetings were liturgical trysts.

As our winter worsened, though, our habits had to change. Wichita Falls, settled just south of the Red River that divided Texas from Oklahoma, and in the storm path we called Tornado Alley, had terrible winters, characterized by bizarre fluctuations of temperature and wicked attacks of sleet and hail. On one of the first really cold days, when we were playing in the basement, I mentioned to my grandmother that kids had asked me where I was going when I went out the door. "Are you crazy?" they said as I pulled on my jacket.

She said, "It's too cold for you to come outside anyway." If she had said, "But you must come out! I have to see you, if only for a moment!" I think I would have braved any weather for a quick clasp of our hands. Instead, she said, "When it's raining or it's cold, you can watch for me, can't you?"

I would have to go into one of the small practice rooms in the basement and climb on a bench and stretch across the top of the piano to see through the ground-level window. I was a little baffled by her question, but soon she made herself clear. She drove her pea-green Studebaker slowly around the block. She made at least three circuits. She raised her right hand over her head, turned so that the fingers were toward me; her waves were like a bridal train, strung out behind her. If I needed her, I could run out and catch her on the second or third time around.

I liked watching for her, and if I forgot—and, astonishingly, I sometimes did—I ran out to see her the next day, to make up for forgetting, no matter what the weather was, and even though she would have had no way to know of my lapsed attention. I learned early the guilt of not appreciating love and sacrifice. Sometimes when she gave me money, she said, "Save it, my precious, you never can tell." Money was a subtle criticism of my parents, and it made me her accomplice in conspiracy, but only she and I knew about it and it pleased her to give to me, and also I thought she might be right.

I called her on Saturday evenings after supper on the students' basement phone. The light was always off, and I didn't think I should turn it on. In winter, it was so dark I had to grope the wall to keep from stumbling. Each week, the mistress of boarders gave me a dime and said, "Don't take too long." In the dim light, completely alone, I could yield to the sense of clandestineness and my self-pity. Before I dialed, and after I hung up, I pressed my forehead against the black phone box, willing our connection, mourning our separation. I told her how much I missed her. I said it was lonely at the convent; I was the only girl who did not go home for the weekend. Her voice cracked like something dry. "Oh my, oh my," she would say. There were long silences. Feeling guilty, I finally told her that the sisters were very nice to me on the weekend. Sometimes one of them played checkers with me. They lent me magazines like *Look* and *Life* that donors had subscribed to for them. Once the two kitchen sisters took me with them into the country, where they bought vegetables. They had been rough farm girls from big families, insulated from higher education, and with them I saw another side of religious life, listening to them complain and joke about the "upstairs nuns." Another time, the principal's niece invited me to lunch with her and her husband at a restaurant, and I had my first filet mignon, a dainty piece of meat girdled by bacon. None of this measured up to my grandmother's house, of course.

In May, an opportunity came along to see her away from the convent. The Catholic church had arranged for one of the downtown theaters to have a special showing, a double feature, of movies that celebrated Our Holy Mother, whose month was May. The movies were *The Song of Bernadette,* about the appearance of Mary to a girl in Lourdes, France, and *The Miracle of Our Lady of Fatima.* The movies were being shown from ten to two on a Saturday. Students would meet at school and be transported by a special bus. For a dollar, we would see the movies, and during a break at noon, we would be given cheese sandwiches and a Coke.

I didn't think I would be missed in the melee of the lunch break, and so I told my grandmother to come downtown around a quarter to twelve, and to park on a side street by the theater. I would slip away, and sit with her in the car. I might be able to sit out the whole second movie. I had thought about it obsessively. I would miss lunch, I told my grandmother, so she should bring sandwiches for us to share. Or maybe we could drive to the hamburger stand that had corn dogs. She didn't say anything, and I kept adding details to the plan. I even told her the story of Fatima and the scary third secret.

I was nervous because she had not yet agreed to our rendezvous. "You'll come, won't you?" I asked. "I'll be out there looking for you."

"I can't, I can't, oh, oh," she said.

"But why not? Why not?"

"Your mother forbids it."

"My mother won't know anything about it!"

"She's your mother. She has the say."

I couldn't believe it. I went from feverish excitement to cold anger, and hung up without saying I love you.

Still, when the day came and we students went off to the theater, I was back to my old self and I was sure that she would not be able to stay away. I left my seat once before the Bernadette movie was over and went to the bathroom, then sneaked out to the sidewalk and looked up and down the street. At lunch, I took a sandwich, just in case, and then went outside. I turned to the right and went around the block until I was again in front of the theater. I crossed the street and went around the facing block. She hadn't come. I was so upset I thought I might vomit. I threw the sandwich into a bin on the street. When I tried to re-enter the theater, an employee in tight pants and a fancy weskit stopped me and said I could not come in. I protested, but he said once I left, I was, as he put it, "out of luck." He was a high-school boy, all puffed up with authority. "Them's the rules," he said, "even for R.C.'s."

I began to cry in earnest and told him to go and find one of the adults from inside. He smirked, but he did as I asked. One of the mothers came out, took one look at me, and assumed that I had taken ill. She went to find another chaperone, one who had not come on the bus and who had her own car. That mother took me back to the convent, where she turned me over to the sister who had door duty, and I was put to bed for the rest of the afternoon. (A sick girl was always given a jug of water, a small basin for vomiting, and a big bell to ring in an emergency.)

I lay on my bed for hours, thinking of terrible things to say to my grandmother. I did not call her that night. But we never mentioned the botched meeting, or the grudge between her and Mother, either. On Monday she was at the fence, as if nothing had happened. I hadn't expected her; she had to have traded shifts in order to come.

She asked me if I had enjoyed the movies. I said they were very good movies and I hoped some day she would get to see them, too. Even though it wasn't Friday, she gave me a dollar. I kissed her cool dry cheek and told her I loved her. She held my face with the palms of her hands.

"You'll be going home soon," she said. Although she spoke in a neutral tone, I knew immediately that she was saying something more than those words. I always spent part of the summer at my aunt's house, and my mother couldn't stop my grandmother from being there. You had to let my mother have her way until she lifted her ban, out of forgiveness or boredom, or until she needed her mother for herself, but in summer, she would overlook my grandmother's arrangements. In the end, it was easier for her that way.

As it turned out, I did spend one weekend with my grandmother in her house just before school was out. I was running a fever and had a sore throat. I kept feeling that I might throw up, and each false alarm caused me to be nearly hysterical. The mistress of boarders called my grandmother to come and get me. I think she was afraid she wouldn't be able to put me on the bus to Odessa as directed, and I would interfere with the plans the sisters had for themselves once school was out.

My grandmother arrived within half an hour. By evening I was completely well. I thought it was amazing how things worked out. If she had come to meet me, it would have been a sin of disobedience for me. I would have had to confess it. This way, I had the crushing disappointment (to punish me for my devious planning) and then God lifted it and here I was!

SHE TOOK VACATION IN JULY and I saw her at Aunt Mae's and then in Odessa, too, at our house. Mother had been baby-sitting seven children under six. My grandmother had a fit when she saw that. They ended up in a screaming argument about Mother's good sense and her health and my grandmother's compulsion to run other people's lives. Nevertheless, there was no real rift this time. The anger didn't last, maybe because my grandmother was right—Mother would wear out watching little kids—but Mother would have a year or so when she led a more or less normal life, babies and all.

She used the baby-sitting money to defray the higher rent, but she did other things, too. She bought a piano for me and arranged for me to take lessons in music theory with an instructor at the junior college during the month of July. I rode my bike to see him, coming home with long assignments that I loved. He listened to some of my compositions, too, and made suggestions, and helped me write them down.

Toward the end of the summer she decided to give up the baby-sitting, and we moved to a smaller house. She had begun attending Mass at the Mexican church and she assisted in the church's day-care, picking up Spanish at an astonishing rate. I often accompanied her, and several times I made a huge bowl of potato salad and took it to the small trailer where two tiny nuns from Mexico lived. They traveled around the region, visiting homes and teaching Catechism where there was no church. When I gave them the food they always giggled, like girls. I think they probably didn't speak any English.

I liked Odessa. Table-flat, with wide streets and right-angle grids, it was easy to navigate on a bicycle, and I had more freedom than I had ever had. I often rode to the library and spent the afternoon browsing the stacks. I went downtown and wandered through the stores. I met a girl at church, Rita Boosalis, and she became the first close friend I ever had. Every morning I rode my bike across town to the 7:00 Mass, out of habit and pride. There was a small electric organ and I often played it.

Rita and I went swimming, posing for the junior-high boys, who belly flopped and dunked one another and never looked our way. Where Rita was all round, I was straight. We tittered with self-consciousness and assured one another that boys did not matter. I often spent the night at her house. I stood around while she cleaned the tiny house, and then we made chocolate-chip cookies or a no-bake pie. She was studying dance and she taught me stretches and ballet positions.

I told my mother, "It would be okay here if I stayed," but I knew I didn't have a say.

FOUR

I was learning that men are occasions of sin. Even boys are dangerous, because the morals of girls are fragile, like the shells of baby birds. At the Academy of Mary Immaculate, we eighth graders had a one-day spiritual retreat on an April day that came up hot as August. We sat in the school chapel, our heads steaming under wool berets. The visiting priest was a good-looking young man, but we saw him only as priest and waited for him to tell us something we did not already know, beyond the rote rhythms of Catechism.

I sat up, eagerly attentive. The year had been a threshold for me. I had inched my way past the childish, recitative practice of devotions, struggling to discover or invent a more personal practice of my faith, something that I thought of as "more real." I had been influenced by the presence of a new boarder, Bonnie, a senior girl from a farming town who was going to go straight into the Fort Worth novitiate in June. She already lived more like one of the sisters than like a student, rising earlier than the rest of us to go to chapel, and joining the sisters for Matins (morning prayers) and Vespers (evening prayers).

None of the other older girls had any patience with me, but during free time after supper Bonnie sometimes asked me if I wanted to play catch or shoot baskets, and when the weather turned cold, I was comfortable enough with her to sit and talk. By winter I had got up my nerve to tell her that I was frustrated because I didn't know what I was supposed to do when I went to chapel at times other than services. She asked me why I went, and I said because I wanted the company. She patted my knee and said that was fine, God had a big ear. She suggested that I talk silently as if I were on the phone, and then after a while she thought the phone would fade away and I would feel God's presence and it would seem more natural just to say what was on my mind, knowing that I was being heard. Then, she said, I would learn, in time, that I could sit in silence with an open heart and listen. For what? I asked. She took my hand and squeezed it gently. I don't know, she said. It depends on what He has to say to you.

Before long I became comfortable with the silence of the chapel and stopped thinking that something had to happen. It was such a beautiful room, just across the hall from the room where we studied. It always smelled of wax and something else, something I identified with the smell of the sisters. Once in a while Bonnie would come in and sit down beside me for a little while and then we would go out together. She made me feel less lonely. I wonder if I was a project for her, an act of charity.

WE WERE DIVIDED at the retreat, boys and girls—this was the last year boys could attend AMI before enrolling in public schools—so all day we paraded past one another, alternating lectures, prayers, snacks, and silent recreation (walks around the periphery of the grounds). Segregation allowed the introduction of topics that might be inappropriate in mixed company. I don't remember who explained this, but there was no need to belabor it. A retreat was, by its very definition, special, with special rules, and this was our first experience on a higher plane; two days without boys would not bother us. Except for Denny McMurtry, who was smarter than any of us in math, any boy in our class could be bested by almost any girl. We worked harder; we cared more. We shed the boys with a sigh of superiority, then inclined toward Father's instruction.

We heard about God's intentions for women: marriage and motherhood, or the convent—nothing new there. My mind wandered. I counted weeks until I would go to West Texas and see my family. I played the piano in my head, feeling the pulse of notes in my fingers on my thighs. Then something the priest mentioned ignited me. He said, *We have to keep our souls open like windows waiting for the breeze that will carry God's call to us.* He meant a religious vocation. God's beckoning, he said, would come quietly, *like a faint stirring of leaves.* (Saints struck down in the road had been extraordinary cases, with minds so large it took a violent storm to knock them into humility and faith.) We mustn't be too busy, our minds cluttered with thoughts of beauty, boys, movies, or music. (Hair and makeup! His chin quivered with contempt. I can't help wondering if he had some premonition of rock and roll. "Party Doll" would pound us in less than a year with its seductive lyrics: *I want to make love to you, to you.*) We had to keep our heads cocked in case we were called. He hastened to say that those girls who grew up and became wives and mothers would be embracing a holy vocation, too. (He said *wivesnmothers,* there could not be one without the other.)

I lost track of what he said during the rest of that session; I could not stop thinking of the open window. His very words—*window, stirring leaves*—made my heart pound. It was the same feeling that came over me when I knew I had to write. A scrap of poetry (sorry rhymes), a story (fat with sentiment), such things sometimes arrived like a letter to my door. There had been times I had feigned illness in order to bundle up on my bed and scribble through the school day. This was the first time, however, that the inspiration had been for an essay. Oh, I was a good student writer, and I had hardly ever seen a red mark on my papers, but academic compositions were dutiful displays demanded by adults and evaluated by the absence of errors. This was altogether new. This was an urgent need to *argue* something, and my excitement came from the sudden awareness that what I thought I had not thought before *and maybe no one else had either.* I did not yet have the concept of the muse; I thought God, in some mysterious way, had whispered in my ear. I thought it was what you got on retreat. A party favor, for paying attention.

I decided to enter the diocesan essay contest. The topic was vocations and the deadline was a mere three days away. The principal had asked me every day for the past two weeks why I wasn't

entering. She said that Denny McMurtry had done so, and so had
Madeline Laherty, in the high-school division. The school was
counting on me. I could only reply that I had nothing to say. Even
though I had been professing for a couple of years now that I wanted
to be a nun—specifically, a Benedictine nun, to please my mother—
the topic of vocations had not interested me. Everything about it
was so obvious.

In every graduating class there was at least one girl who fas-
tened on the notion of the convent, someone pious who was
known never to sass or disobey. Then, too, recruiters came from
various religious orders once a year to talk to us about vocations (in
the narrowest sense), and they were known to sway a girl who had
not yet made up her mind. My classmate Mozelle Chambers,
barely fourteen years old, had already sworn to enter the Ursulines
four years hence, won over by an afternoon's visit with a persuasive advocate. Now, though, I thought that one might hear God's
call *directly,* and that the call might be particular to oneself. To me.
Like Saint Joan of Arc, called to dress like a boy and save France.
Like Mother's patron saint, Edith, a tenth-century king's daughter
who proved you could be beautiful—decked out in finery—and be
pure and holy, too.

The saint I knew and loved best was the recently canonized
Maria Goretti, who as a girl only eleven years old had died defending her purity in an assault by a boy from a neighboring farm. Of
course I loved her! *She could be me.* She was a saint of my century.
Smitten like millions of girls all over the world, I had recently chosen her for my confirmation namesake. I had a clear picture in my
mind of her heaped on the back of a farmer's wooden cart. I
thought that her holiness lay not just in her virginity (after all, I
was a virgin and hardly holy at all), and not just in her violent death

(people are murdered every day), but in her generosity (*I pray he will repent!*), and especially in the way she saw clearly what she had to do. Her vocation had been martyrdom and she had welcomed her bloody death. I am appalled now to remember thinking of this eleven-year-old peasant girl as capable of such self-aggrandizing projection—in the moments of a brutal attack, no less!—but not only was I immature, I was a Catholic girl in 1956 and was enthralled with the concept of holy purity. The hagiographers were pushing hard this child who had died for virtue, and I simply couldn't conceive of a girl around my age being so good, so brave, and so full of conviction, that she would act *without having to think about it.*

I thought that what had made Maria brave was her belief that she had been blessed with her violent fate, *as my mother had been blessed with her afflictions.* I loved that word, *afflictions.* (That night I would write Mother these thoughts, and she would answer that I had made her weep with pride and love.) Those brave, good girls who were martyred for their faith (Cecelia, Agnes, Perpetua) *had been at that window when God called.* Simple acceptance—that was how you learned to do the right thing, even if you didn't understand everything about what you embraced. Somehow acceptance became faith; your patience and humility got you God's prize—bestowed, not won (Sainthood!). It was heady, romantic stuff, a kind of Prince Charming story in which God himself came along to rescue you, not from death, but from anonymity. I was thrilled by the simple virtue of having a fresh thought of my own at age twelve. I wasn't mature enough to turn around and evaluate it, too.

I wish there had been someone to tell me on the spot how naïve I was, that it is possible to do everything you are "supposed to do" and gain nothing. That Maria was a victim perfect for her time, an icon of Catholic sexual politics.

That a girl waiting for a prince—even God—is a person of no moral consequence.

AT LUNCH I SAT against the fence away from the other girls, eating salted peanuts one by one from a tiny bag. The sky was low, a dirty yellow color smudged with gritty dust. I thought of my grandmother standing in her yard across town, her hand at her eyes, predicting rain or hail or maybe just turning her face to the wind. I would have liked to sit at a real window in one of the quiet front parlors and watch the weather change. I wanted to skip the rest of the day's schedule and give myself over to the pictures in my mind, and to words. (How like *faint stirrings!*) But I considered the essay—whole somewhere inside me, but blurry, as if through a delicate membrane—a gift, and if I lied to gain time, I might lose it. Reluctantly, I stood and brushed dust from my skirt and went to stand in line.

In the last session, Father spoke about sex. I was disappointed. I was not interested. The sisters had not discussed sex with us, nor had our parents. We still played children's games at recess (hop-scotch, jump rope, convent) and shied away, girls from boys. But Father was determined to catch us before we sinned. He ignored our tittering. I didn't think he had much sense of who we were. Sin, for us, was almost always something we said: gossip, inso-lence, jeers. It had nothing to do with what was beneath our skirts. We bent our heads, though, suddenly modest as a covey of postu-lants. We bore his prattle. He said that we were still very young and he was sure our parents did not let us go out unsupervised, but he knew that one day soon we would feel "stirrings" and we would look at boys in a different way. We would be *tempted*.

It was inconceivable to me. I had other plans, vague but high-minded. (I recognized that that word, *stirrings,* was the same one he had used to describe God's whispers through the window. I thought the word, used first about God and then about boys, was now meaningless, a sign of Father's imprecision and fallibility.) He said we must protect our innocence, but we might not know how subtle were the ways of boys seeking knowledge of our "womanly secrets." (I didn't think he had taken a close look at our boys, either.) I was sitting next to Mozelle Chambers, and she reached out and squeezed my hand. She was an earnest and humorless girl, so I knew it wasn't to suppress laughter. She was scared; she wanted my support. Already her breasts were like pillows she smashed into halter bras. I squeezed back. Father told us sex could scar our womanhood and mar our souls. At the end, almost in afterthought, he said that it was a mortal sin to French-kiss outside of marriage. Then he led us in three Hail Marys and declared our retreat over.

As we filed out, hot and tired and overinstructed, I had an image in my mind that confused Maria Goretti and myself: I saw my own body torn and slung on a cart to no good, for I would never embrace martyrdom, never forgive my persecutor; I would never ascend to goodness.

THE PRINCIPAL, Sister Mary John, came to tell me my essay's fate. She took me into the kitchen and gave me a bottle of Coca-Cola, a special treat. I sat across from her, sipping nervously, wondering what I had done wrong. She would probably be my teacher next year, and it was important that she approved of me in every way. I liked her because she didn't condescend to us, and I looked forward to her freshman Religion and Ethics class, in which we would be thoroughly trained as *adult* Catholics. I had heard that she talked about things like "scruples" and "mysticism," topics that sounded intriguing and challenging. I did not doubt that my mother would send me back for high school, and in a way these sisters had become family to me.

Sister said she hadn't had an opportunity to talk to me lately and she wanted to hear how my mother was doing. I told her about the little Mexican boy Mother was keeping. His name was Davy. Sister nodded; Mother had written to her about him.

Sister had placed me in a high-school French class and she wondered if I had enjoyed it. Although the truth was that I had felt out of place with the older girls, I assured her that I loved French. I even mentioned that I would like to go to Lourdes some day. I wanted her to be glad to have done special things for me.

When I had drained the last of the pop, she rinsed and wiped the bottle and put it in a wooden case in the corner. She sat back down and put her hands over mine on the tabletop.

"I spent quite a morning on the phone with the bishop's office," she said, "and all because of your essay." She did not looked pleased, and I guessed that I was about to be made unhappy. She shifted, and I had a sudden awareness of her girth, of how her large buttocks would go out past the stool.

Both Denny and Madeline had won first prizes in their divisions. I wasn't surprised. Everyone knew how smart they were, and that they had effective personal points to make. Denny, a child in a large family, had two sisters who were nuns, and a brother soon to be ordained. Madeline would graduate in a few weeks and then would become a postulant—a trainee nun—in the Carmelite order in Fort Worth. I said I was glad that they had won, while I blinked to keep from crying. I knew Sister must be pleased; she emphasized writing from the earliest grades.

She went on. "I asked about you. I just couldn't believe you hadn't placed. Your composition went far beyond platitudes. It was *abstract*. And yet it didn't surprise me; I told them that. It demonstrated a certain leap, but it was not unlike other work of yours. Say that nice essay you wrote about the Soviet Union and the dangers of appeasement. There was a lot of hemming and hawing, but I can be very pushy. Finally someone told me that they felt a child of thirteen could not have written such a provocative essay. Of course I told them you are twelve!"

"Did I do something wrong?"

"I told them you are the best writer we've ever had, and that you most certainly would not have plagiarized. They said that someone had helped you. I suggested they try to find such a passage in any book they knew."

"But I wrote it the day of the retreat! Sitting in the sophomore homeroom, waiting for supper. I wrote it by myself."

"Of course you did." She squeezed my hands. "And I worked my way up until I found someone who could understand. That you live with us. That you had no one to assist you." She rearranged herself, putting her hands back in their hiding place inside her habit. She seemed to be waiting for me to digest what she had said so far. When I said nothing, she said that the bishop's office had accepted her defense of me. Before I could exhale the excited breath I took just past her words, she added, "But they had already notified the other winners."

I began to cry. Sister drew out a large pressed white handkerchief and gave it to me. She said that she and the bishop's office had worked out an agreement about me. There were two awards in each of four categories, boys and girls, elementary and secondary. But in the elementary girls group, I would be recognized, too, with a "special commendation." I would receive the same prize as the first-place winner: $10 in savings stamps. The ceremony was the following Saturday.

I sniffled.

"You'll want to dress up," she said. "We'll go to Fort Worth for the ceremony in the co-cathedral. You'll walk down a long aisle, and kiss the bishop's ring. It's an honor. You must try to see this as a special lesson in humility, child."

I nodded, but I desperately wanted to go back and fix the essay. How could my ideas have excited me so much and been all wrong? *How could I have been so happy?* Suddenly I realized how much my writing meant to me. It was from some place inside me, where I was not pretending to be smart or good or holy, where I simply *was*. I wished I had kept my thoughts about Maria Goretti to myself. I wished fervently not to have been named at all. I did not want to walk down an aisle in front of people for the rigged commendation; what would they think, to see me receiving consolation, as if I were a very sick child, or a very slow one? At best, they would think it was third place. I did not want to say "Thank you." The ceremony would be a lesson, not in humility, but in humiliation.

SISTER TOOK ME TO TOWN to buy new pumps, the first pair of shoes I had ever had with a heel. They gave me something to focus on at the ceremony. They gave me something to feel proud of. I must have seemed a solemn girl, planting my steps with great care like a bride, making my way to the altar and the bishop. I have a photograph of the three of us AMI students. It was taken at the altar after the ceremony. Madeline is serene and pretty in a two-piece suit. Denny, ruddy faced and wearing too-short pants, is grinning and looking away from the camera toward his family. I am in the middle, wearing a dark cotton print dress with an A-line skirt that sweeps almost to my ankles—my grandmother had made it for me the year before—and a tiny pillbox hat. I am glum as can be and unable to hide it. I seem to be studying a spot on the floor. I remember I was hungry and that the heels of my feet were sore where the shoes rubbed.

I received the promised savings stamps, but no medal. After the ceremony Sister Mary John and I, with Madeline and AMI's high-school English teacher, Sister Sebastian, drove to Our Lady of Victory Academy in Fort Worth to have lunch with several of the sisters. One of the teachers there, Sister Paula Thérèse, showed me all around the school. It was a massive, red-brick structure, five stories high. It had the solid look of castles and cathedrals, sitting as it did in the middle of a full city block, surrounded by tended grounds, a grotto, and gardens of flowers and vegetables. As we walked before lunch along the hallway to a bathroom, Madeline said to me, "How grand these convents are." She sounded disapproving and aloof, and I realized I neither admired nor liked her, although I envied her for knowing how her life would go from now on. In her essay, she had said that she had no thought of the future beyond that moment when she passed through the door of the Carmelite convent and relinquished her will to God. She made a vocation sound like anesthesia.

At the door as we were leaving, Sister Paula Thérèse said she was looking forward to seeing me again. She had a beautiful mouth. Had she ever been kissed? She looked like a nun in a movie, someone who would win the hearts and souls of heathens for God, simply because they would swoon to please her. I was so fixated on her beauty, I didn't really notice what she had said.

I POURED MYSELF into daily practice for my piano recital—before and after school, between supper and study hall. I was playing a difficult piece by Grieg, a Bach cantata, a Chopin nocturne, and two compositions of my own. I knew that Denny, who would have his recital on the day after mine, was playing noisy, showy pieces, like Beethoven's "Appassionata," and a crowd-pleaser by Rachmaninoff. Many of the same people would come to both days; of course they would compare us. I had to be precise, nuanced, confident. We were a complementary pair, like table lamps. My hands would arch perfectly, so that my knuckles were high and white. His hands would be spread wide and flat, he would pound the keys.

The recital was held on a Wednesday afternoon at four. My family could not afford to come from West Texas, of course. Everyone worked, and I would be home soon anyway, and I would play all my pieces on my very own piano. My grandmother had promised to try, but her appearance was dependant on her schedule, and possibly on her ability to switch shifts. Mother ordered an orchid that was delivered to me that morning. A few hours later, another one arrived, this one from my grandmother, and I burst into tears. Sister Francis Joseph soothed me. She said I would wear Mother's flower that afternoon, and my grandmother's at Mass on Sunday.

Most of the sisters came to the recital, and so did one of the priests (Father Daly was out of town), the housekeeper from the rectory, and a number of parents and students, including all the boarders. The sisters had ordered a large wicker basket of flowers to sit on the stage. I was just offstage, taking deep breaths and waiting for the minute hand to hit the mark, when Sister came to tell me that my grandmother was in the back of the room. Sister said, "She won't come in and sit down. She says she's on her way to work."

I stepped from the wings and held my hands together at my waist. I looked to the door, and there was my grandmother, as Sister had said. She was wearing her work clothes, her head wrapped in a white cloth. She clasped her hands below her breasts. I caught her eye, and she smiled and blew me a kiss. My chest flooded with relief and love, and I crossed the stage, sat down, and arranged my starchy dress on the bench. I played perfectly. The boarders clapped loudly and one of them foolishly called out, "Bravo!" and made the others laugh. I bowed, and looked toward the door, but she was gone. I knew, though, that she was proud of me. She would tell all the girls at work: *You ought to hear her play.*

A FEW DAYS LATER, I was in study hall when Sister Mary John came to talk to me again. We went into another classroom and sat down, almost knee to knee.

"You must know how dear you have been to us," she said. "And you must know how we have tried to challenge you and give you a good education."

"Yes," I said timidly. I thought she was making a reference to my recital. "I practiced very hard, Sister."

She patted my knee. "Now I think you should go to school in Fort Worth. Victory can offer you much more than we can. Our finest music teacher is there. She could have been a concert pianist if she had not answered God's call. There is a forensics program, a newspaper, drama. I have talked to your mother."

"I'm going home, though, aren't I? For the summer?" School would be out in a few days. I had a sudden panicky fear that the nuns were simply going to pass me from hand to hand. I had been replaced by Mother's little brown foster child. Mother had sent a photograph of him and bragged about how smart he was.

"Of course you'll go home," Sister said. "But in the fall, you will be a Victory girl." I could see that she was enormously pleased.

When I didn't say anything, she said, "There will be more girls there, it will be like a big family. Do you have any questions?"

"I do have a question, Sister," I said, thinking only at that moment what I wanted to know. "Could you tell me what was wrong with my essay?"

She sighed and straightened her apron, tugging at it and then tucking her hands inside her sleeves. "I believe they were surprised by your suggestion that Saint Maria Goretti had a choice that day, and that she chose martyrdom because it was her vocation. There is an implication that some martyrs may have been victims with no wills of their own, and may not have merited their special rewards."

"I didn't say anything about *other* martyrs. I don't *care* about them!" The conversation was quickly going over my head.

"Religious people sometimes think too hard about the simplest things, but they are very surprised when a young person pursues a mystery," Sister said. "You could be a very good girl, you know, if you won't let your pride nettle you too much."

I stayed in my chair, staring at the top of the desk. In my lap, my fists were tight balls. "I would freeze up, I'd be so scared. I would let him do whatever he wanted, because I wouldn't want to die. I would go to confession later, just to be sure." I looked up defiantly.

Sister made the sign of the cross hastily and glared at me. "The prideful part is letting too much into your head. You must ask the Holy Ghost to send a gust now and then to blow away your fancies."

That stupid breeze again. I said I would. And I did, for years and years, until long after I stopped praying for anything else at all.

I WAS PACKED and my suitcases were in the front parlor. Daddy was coming for me soon after lunch. I was the only boarder left. Sister Mary John had given me a big hug after morning Mass. Skinny old Sister Thecla had given me a little brown paper bag of candy for the trip. Now the mistress of boarders wanted to take my picture. She said she would send copies to my mother when they were developed. We went outside and she took a photograph of me sitting on the steps, and another standing among the rosebushes. I was wearing a dressy dress with puffed sleeves and a plaid taffeta skirt.

When we were done, Sister gave me a dollar and sent me across the street and over to the corner hamburger stand for my lunch, a special treat, but the smell of frying meat made me queasy. I had French fries and a cherry Coke and I walked slowly back. It was very hot and still. Before I entered the building again,

I looked up and down the streets. I had told my grandmother that I would leave today, and I had assumed that she would come to say goodbye.

I went to the restroom and then back into the parlor to wait. I went straight to the corner of the room, where I could look out windows on two sides. I simply knew that she would be there.

She was parked at the corner. She wasn't looking at the building. She didn't know when I would leave, or if I had already gone. Both of her arms rested on the steering wheel and her head lay against the window, to her left, away from me. I scratched at the pane. I whispered her name. She did not move. In a little while, she drove away.

IT WAS SUMMER before I had the opportunity to ask my mother to explain to me what a French kiss was. I tried to ask her casually, as if I were merely clearing up some small matter. "Something came up at school," I said. "We had a retreat." Then I asked.

Her response—she was ironing in the kitchen, a fan blowing hot air on us—was amused and tender and rather daintily vague. "Just tell me!" I said. She finished pressing the sleeves of a blouse, hung it on a hanger on a hook over the back of the door, and unplugged the iron. All the while I watched, frenzied by her silence. She told me to pour iced tea for us, she would be through in a minute. She put the plastic bag, with its burden of damp, rolled clothes, back on the bottom shelf of the refrigerator where she stored it until she had time to iron. She said what we needed was to sit where it was cool and enjoy our drinks.

"Let's go in the bedroom," she said. The two bedrooms each

had a window air conditioner, called a "swamp cooler," and Mother hardly ever turned hers off, since she never knew when one of us would want to lie down. Every few hours one of us had to go outside and use a hose to soak the strawlike matting that encased the unit. When we went back later, the sandy ground beneath the window would be completely dry again.

The door to the tiny room I shared with my sister was closed, because she was napping. On my bed was Davy, the little Mexican boy my mother had been keeping most of that school year. He was just a toddler, maybe a year and a half old, and he slept at night on a crib mattress on the floor in her room; he followed her like a puppy all day and never cried. I thought Mother babysat Davy because the Mexican priest, Father Dominguez, whom she admired greatly, had asked her to do so. Davy was cute but foreign—as much for being male as for being Mexican—and all in all, did not seem important. He was somebody else's dark little boy, and luckily for him Mother was neither ill nor employed just then.

We sat on my parents' bed, propped side by side against the padded vinyl headboard. Sometimes, when it was too hot to bear, we would spend whole afternoons in here, sprawled out with books and magazines, writing tablets, paper dolls, crayons and coloring books, the odd toy. Mother wrote dreamily in stenographers' notebooks that had pale green pages with a faint red line down the middle. She kept the books, each one bound shut by a rubber band, in a box from a dress shop. Davy, naked except for little white britches over his diaper, always wanted to be next to her, but he couldn't be still for long unless he fell asleep. More than once Daddy came home and found us in a dozing pile. He always laughed, *Har, har,* like a bad actor in a play.

My mother and I settled in like girlfriends. Our bare legs, spotty with chill-bumps, stuck out from our shorts. I sipped my tea and shook the sweating glass to make the ice rattle. I was twelve years old, soon to be thirteen. I thought of myself as a grown-up inside a small body, but truly I was innocent in a way most American children no longer are; there had been almost no television and few movies. (Catholics were bound by a ponderous rating system that shut children out of almost everything.) My "free reading" that year had included *The Silver Chalice, Ramona* (twice), *Cheaper by the Dozen, Mother's Bank Account, The Miracle of the Bells,* and numerous biographies of saints. My favorite novel of all time was about a vestal virgin in ancient Rome. People did not curse in public, and the worst expletive I had heard in my family was "I'll be dipped" (only the men said it). I not only didn't know any dirty words, I don't think I had ever heard any popular slang at all. I knew that sex was what mothers and fathers did in the dark to make babies and I suppose I had some faint notion of what it involved, but I had never considered the *details*—whose legs were where, whether it hurt, how long it took. I was hot with embarrassment, but I was greedy for information. The way we were seated, we did not have to look at each other. Very carefully, but with an edge of nonchalance—*Hey, it's not such a big deal!*—Mother filled me in.

I got the picture. Although I didn't say anything, the disgust I felt burned my cheeks. I had imagined Saint Maria Goretti's torment as something fumbled and vulgar, complicated by the horror of a knife, but I knew her fate in the Italian countryside many years ago would never be my own. A hot and sloppy French kiss was something possible, however; even, some might think, to be expected down the line. It was not forced on you, it was something you wanted, "when the time was right." I looked at my mother with barely suppressed contempt. "And do you like it?"

She ran her hands through her hair and tugged at it. "I have liked it," she said, nearly whispering, and I was smart enough to know when I hadn't been given a straight answer. Her evasion made my stomach knot. I knew it had to do with Daddy, with how much she loved him, or didn't.

"Don't you worry, sweetie," she said, leaning toward me to dab at my wet lips. She was so close, she might easily have kissed me. "You'll understand these things one day. You'll have feelings you know nothing about right now." She tucked my hair back behind my ears. The light caress of her cool fingers was unbearably sweet. Was I such a baby, to crave my mother's touch?

"It's odd that a priest would have brought up the subject just yet." There was the hint of a smile on her face. "Was he cute?"

I drew back furiously. How could she have forgotten the times we had knelt together and recited from her little prayer book, *Moments with God:* "Because you hate sin so much, sweet Mother Mary, keep us far away from dangerous occasions, help us to avoid temptations."

She knew she had provoked me. "Don't be so serious."

I always had to have the last word. "Even if I fall in love," I said, "even if I get married—and I don't think those things will ever happen—I am never, ever, going to French-kiss." Mother was right about one thing: it was funny that Father worried about us. He didn't know much about girls like us. Girls from Mary Immaculate.

"Some things," I said, and licked my upper lip, "are *private*." I gave her a mean look before I jumped up and went to the kitchen with my glass. Then I went outside to ride my bicycle in the awful heat. I went around and around the block, too hot and upset to plot a route. Our neighborhood looked like it was going back to prairie; the small run-down houses were set back with weedy, stickery patches in front. Nobody was out. There were no trees. In any direction, I saw blue-white sky. I could never ride far enough to find a hill, standing water, or a bed of flowers. Pedaling crazily, I bent over, head down, as if studying the street for scars. As if I were trying to find an open place, a fissure into which I could fall. After a while I glanced up in passing, and I saw my mother standing in the doorway behind the screen, watching for me, one hand up flat on the mesh. When I came around again, she was still there. She had cracked the door open, just enough so that sunlight glinted on the brassy gold of her hair. I saw her, and I knew that she was remembering kisses like the ones I had asked about, and that she was thinking about me one day with kisses of my own. Oh, I don't say that I thought those things exactly so; it was more a welling up in me of sadness and pity that there was such a gulf between us. This was what it meant to be a child, I thought: to see the stretch of a future in front of me, while my mother's opportunities dwindled. I forgave her instantly for taunting me with the mysteries of adulthood, then treating me like a child. In time I would forget her tenderness and imagine her legacy to me as nothing more than bad example. But on that day I tamped down my grudges and forgave her everything, just for being there when I rode by. Years later I would think of her at the door and I would see her again in my mind's eye. It took me much longer to remember the child on the bicycle, sick at the thought of a man's tongue in her mouth, in love with no one yet but her mother.

FIVE

Victory girls snapped to. We walked in lines like cadets. We stood to answer questions, holding our hands cupped at our waists. We had a protocol for everything: genuflections as we entered a pew; greetings as we passed the sisters in the halls; papers inscribed at the top of each page, *JMJ,* to stand for *Jesus, Mary, Joseph.* Our suits were navy blue wool, the skirt below the knee. In chapel we wore lengths of stiff blue netting held to our heads by narrow bands, except on feast days when we wore berets. Only seniors wore lipstick.

Boarders' lives after the school day was done were accounted for and supervised. We ate in assigned chairs and studied for prescribed hours. Anything that interrupted routine required special permission. At eight we closed our books and went upstairs to bathe in the order posted on the bath-stall doors. At nine we had "quiet hour" that lasted half that long, then lights were out. On Wednesdays we piled our sheets in the hall for the laundry sister and polished our saddle oxfords. We washed our underwear by hand on Saturday morning after breakfast and cleaned the dorm while Sister checked the neatness of our dresser drawers. Weekend afternoons were more relaxed, but we could never leave the grounds. There was no TV. Once a girl's parents invited me to spend the night, and they took me to the Cow Palace to hear Ricky Nelson, but I felt so guilty, I never mentioned it to any of the other girls, or even to my mother. I never shopped or bought a magazine. Our letters were opened, coming and going. This was the only rule that chafed me, and I sent some letters out with friends from my class. How could I let someone read what I wrote my mother? That I was the only girl who did not have periods, and that my nipples itched. That I felt light as beaten egg white after receiving Communion; I could feel myself rise, then drift back down, and for a moment it seemed the chapel floated and I was alone.

There were girls who curled their lips at the rules, who sashayed down the center of the hall instead of to the right, who whispered in study hall and went to detention, but at their worst they were decent students who knew they accomplished little with their rebellion. All in all, the building was a hum of low voices and frequent laughter, soft steps and the sweet sounds of music practice. I had permission for exceptions to some rules. I could always go to practice piano. If I had a headache I could go upstairs to lie down. I could go to the cold locker in the basement to make an ice pack for my head. And after I fainted once, I was encouraged to drink little cans of juice from the locker any time I wanted, morning to night.

My classmates were friendly, sweet, serious girls, and although we formed interest groups, issues of popularity simply did not arise. Some girls were easier than others to like, and some were difficult by nature, but being mean would have been a sin. We worked hard, divided into two classes, moving in clusters through our day's schedule. We were competitive and collegial at the same time, qualities that carried over into debate and other speech events, popular with the best freshman girls. We were ferried to small tournaments at other Catholic schools, spending the night at host homes. Almost every afternoon you could find us in the basement, poring over our evidence cards, jockeying for the best partner assignments.

In this way, my first semester slid by. I had arrived a little scared and immensely lonesome, but my pride and determination to please my mother carried me until I was caught up in habit and the small pleasures of scholarship. I only minded that beautiful Sister Paula Thérèse was homeroom teacher for the other classroom, and that when she cast the first play of the year, *The Boy with a Cart,* she gave the lead (a boy's role) to a sweet, dumpy girl from her class, Shirley, and made the rest of us part of a chorus. Shirley came across as dogged and amiable, exactly right for a boy dragging a cart across the landscape on an errand for God.

I went home at Christmas by train with a packet of A+ essays, drawings, and plenty to tell, but the house was mired in gloom. Mother's Mexican foster child, Davy, was gone. Mother and Daddy had applied for adoption and it would have gone through soon after the new year, but something had happened before the final papers were approved. Mother had cried herself limp, and

Karen looked stricken, too. Only Daddy seemed normal, but when I asked him, he glared and said "He went *home*," which made no sense and was clearly meant to shut me up and off. Our Christmas motions were pitiful. I couldn't wait to go back to Fort Worth.

Karen went with me. She was wide-eyed and compliant, but once we settled in at school, she in a separate dormitory with three other girls her age, she began to cry. She never made any noise or fuss, but just about any time you looked at her she was crying. She did her schoolwork, ate her meals, did her chores, but she was the saddest child I'd ever seen. I went into her dorm to kiss her good-night, feeling impatient to get away again and guilty that I didn't know what to do. After five or six weeks the sisters asked Mother to come get her. When they were gone, I went to bed, imagining them on the road, hoping that Mother would stop somewhere, maybe for gas or coffee, and say, *What was I thinking, I've got to go back! I don't want her to be a Victory girl, I want her to be with me.*

I WENT HOME AT EASTER and clung to Mother. When it was time to return to school, I said I couldn't walk. My legs hurt too much. Dr. Miller came to the house. He said it was growing pains and that I needed calcium and iron. Daddy rubbed my legs while Mother packed my bag. The morning came for me to go and my legs were stiff, straight out; even Daddy couldn't bend them. Dr. Miller gave me a shot that made the room go around. There were phone calls and tears, a bedpan and rubdowns. My teachers sent assignments and the class made a big "get well" card. I began to walk on wobbly legs, but school was almost over and it didn't make sense to journey back and forth again.

Early in June, Sister Paula and my mother talked on the phone for a long time. Was I going to stay at home or not? I voted yes, until Mother told me I had a scholarship to debate camp at the new Catholic university outside Dallas, in July. Of course I would have to promise to be a Victory girl again. I took the bus to Dallas all alone. I loved every moment of the camp. I slept in a private dorm room and ate in a cafeteria with Jesuit boys! I worked on the new debate topic and was in an acting class. My partner and I won the practice tournament.

While I was there, Mother went to a Dallas hospital. One of the instructors drove me in to see her, making me miss an acting class. I was sullen and didn't understand when she talked about her abscesses and the new antibiotics that had cleared them up. Then she said she'd arranged for me to spend a few days in the hospital at the end of camp, for a checkup. I would get to fly home, as reward.

I made a terrible scene. I would be alone, and nothing was wrong! She said I was the smallest girl in the high school. Didn't I want to grow? Didn't I want to be her big girl? I ended up weeping, my arms around her neck.

I took the long cab ride into the city from campus early in the morning. That afternoon they took me into a chilly examining room and propped my legs up for my first ever internal exam. I was terrified, humiliated, and shocked. I made no sound, no movement. After the supper rounds (Jell-O for me, there would be X rays the next day) I dressed and slipped out of the hospital, edging my way along the shadows like a spy. I walked the empty downtown streets while frantic personnel looked for me on every floor. A policeman found me standing in the doorway of a bank. I gave in. I promised Mother I would do what they said.

They told me I was anemic. They named things that I should eat. Sister Rose of Lima, our mistress of boarders, gave me painful B-12 shots every Friday after school, until the day I left Victory for good. I tried to believe that I was not really sick, only special. What I had been through had been good for my soul.

SOMETIMES I WOULD SEE the postulants and novices who were living and training in the building where I too lived. They were in another part, almost hidden away, but I saw them if I got up early to go to 7:00 Mass, and sometimes I heard their sweet voices as they practiced Gregorian chants. They were always moving in a bunch. Once I looked out of my window up on the fifth floor and saw them on the grounds playing Wiffle ball; it was so strange to see them laughing and running around like that. I hadn't thought of them as ever having fun. I thought that part of what they were learning was to be cold and aloof and formal. None of the sisters were unkind, and I realize now that the changes at OLV from what I had experienced at AMI had a lot to do with simple numbers, but I could never have gone to one of them for a hug.

Sister Rose of Lima was a nice enough person, though occasionally cranky, but I had the unhappy habit of analyzing her every word or action of discipline, whether it involved me or not (as it almost never did), so I was almost constantly in a state of low anger toward her. I especially admired Sister Paula Thérèse and craved her approval, but she gave me nothing more than she gave any other girl, even though I was the most successful of all her speech participants. I was afraid of my music teacher, Sister Odilia, who was very tall, with pale blue eyes. And I began to have a problem with her my second year. There simply wasn't enough of me to go around. She was a gifted artist and a strict instructor and she complained to Sister Paula that I was spending too much time on speech and that my music was sliding. Consequently, Sister Paula left me out of a tournament, infuriating me. I had been shamed into practicing all I could, between breakfast and classes, after supper instead of recreation, and so on. But, as I cried when I missed the tournament, *she didn't own me!*

Sister Odilia was preparing me for a state audition, and I suspect she had more than a little of her own ego invested in my performance. She had given me two extraordinarily difficult pieces. I practiced on a baby grand piano in the parlor outside her studio. Between students, she would come out, push me aside and pound out my pieces, shaming me with her ease.

Through all of this, my body was tormenting me in a number of ways. I was obsessed with the fact that I had not begun my periods. I had my little "setup" of pad and belt in my drawer, and I took it with me on my trips. I was always feeling some new abdominal pain that might be "it" but wasn't. I could work myself into nausea and headache just thinking about it. I had no breasts, but I had almost constant soreness and I wore a bra with a flat cup. I had rashes around my knees, obviously due to an allergy to my wool skirts, but no one took note of that and I suffered until I said something to a classmate who mentioned it to her mother, who made me a double-faced slip! At night, I often woke up because I couldn't lie still. I moved around, my legs twitched, my elbows jerked. There were times I could have sworn that I felt my hair at the points it came out of my head. I worried that I was going crazy. Or that the devil was tormenting me. Once for a week or two I became obsessed with the idea that I was getting stigmata, and I prayed that I would get the visible kind so that I would be believed and somebody would help me make them go away.

One night after lights out I came back from the bathroom and I wanted nothing so much as to scream or throw myself out of a window. It was like having poison oak. I threw myself to the floor, face down, arms out. I had some idea that I was giving my suffering to Jesus. My logic was fuzzy; I wasn't really offering it up so much as saying, *Please take this away, you can have it.* The noise of my body slapping down on the wood caught Sister Rose's attention and she ran down to see what had happened. She helped me up to my bed—I whimpered convincingly—and sent a girl to get a damp washcloth for my forehead. She sat on the edge of my bed like a mother. What could I do except claim that I had fainted? That was when I was told to drink all the juice I wanted whenever I wanted, and grab a few crackers, too. After that I could go down to the big walk-in cold locker in the basement for snacks, even before Mass, with a dispensation from the priest on "standing orders."

As long as I had my head in a book or I was caught up in farm subsidies or foreign aid (topics for debate), I didn't have these problems. It was when I stopped thinking logical thoughts, when I stopped walking rote steps, when I had to *feel* something, that it became more than I could contain in my small, anemic, away-from-Mother body. And that included music. It was as if I reached the exact place where playing exceeded what my hands (and head) could do without my whole heart. My music teacher thought that I was lazy and inattentive and unfaithful besides, but I felt myself to be on the edge of an experience that scared me to death. So I found a way to get out of it, a way that had worked that Easter of my freshman year when my stiff legs kept me home with Mother.

One day, I played for about ten minutes and then I noticed that my right ring finger was buckling with a spasm. I rubbed it, I blew on it, I even sat on it. I went back to playing, but it wouldn't stop. I told Sister Odilia, and she said I should use a lighter touch. Another day it was my little finger. My wrists burned and sometimes my right elbow jerked upward halfway to my ear as if I had received an electric shock. Another day I sat down and I couldn't make my fingers touch the keys. I used one fist to pound the other hand, but it stayed stiff an inch above the keyboard as if there were a pane of glass stopping me. I had been practicing Beethoven's "Pathetique," a piece I should have played well enough, and I began sobbing. Sister Odilia came in and told me I was a baby and a put-on. She said she would give me something easier, something I was *up to,* until I *got serious,* but it was all to no good. Relief rose from me like waning fever from the flu. I was giddy with relief. My frozen arms had freed me.

I entered my head. I wrote poems and stories almost daily. My stories were all set in ancient Rome or Greece. I wrote Mother and told her that I felt dizzy when I swallowed the Host at Mass. I told her that I dreamed of Heaven: I was on a houseboat, floating on a river of gilt.

EVERY MORNING I ROSE in the dark to go to Mass with the sisters and the sisters in training. Sometimes one of the older schoolgirls went with me, but often I was the only boarder. I sat behind the sisters; I didn't want them to think I was showing off. I didn't want them to notice me at all. If I could have attended in a private box, behind a grille, that would have suited me fine. I went early because it was hard to do, hard to get up in the dark, and I wanted to do what was hard. I craved the Host. I hungered for Christ. There's no other way to say it. It was another obsession. Perhaps it connected to my Mother, with whom I had received Communion so many times. Perhaps it was my way of clinging to a sense of specialness, of connectedness. Of Christness. It was passion. I wanted Christ to sweep me away. In my little world, this castle on an acre, I fretted and itched and ached and whined, but in the chapel I could believe that I was capable of calming down and submitting myself to him. It was a child's illogical mix of pride and humility.

Our religious instruction was not remarkable for its deep thinking. Mostly, we memorized and recited. But concepts worked their ways into me and I struggled with them, converting them to something that made sense to me at my age, in my circumstances. Catholic children in those days didn't read the Bible, except for the passages presented in the daily Mass, so we didn't interpret for ourselves the meaning of Christ's actions, but I'm sure I wasn't the only thoughtful young girl to sort out a Christ to fit her needs.

I knew that I was vain and selfish and impatient, and I wanted a Jesus that was forgiving. I was weak and needy and lonely and I wanted a Jesus that loved me as a child but also as one struggling to grow up. I was proud and willful, but I wanted Jesus to help me keep my pride to myself and use it to do the right things. I asked both Sister Paula and Sister Rose for books to help me grow spiritually but they told me that my religious classes were carefully planned for that purpose and that I was getting ahead of myself. A priest came in on Saturdays for confession, but I didn't know him and didn't feel I could approach him with the same kind of question.

I knew two things to do. In my studies I had been taught the concept of "close reading," in which we were told to read a line or a paragraph several times and to paraphrase it and then to say it more concisely, compressing its meaning. In this way we could work our way through an important passage and get more out of it. So I would sometimes take something from that day's reading at Mass and come back to it later and try to rethink it. Most of the time this ended up being a kind of elaboration that was a lot like composing a narrative or example, but it was a sort of clumsy meditation. Other times, I did what I had learned from Bonnie in eighth grade: I just sat and waited for God to tell me something. What I liked about that, over time, was the calm that came with it, even if I cried. It was typical of me to approach praying as if I had to match a standard, but ultimately the best moments were the empty ones, when the roar of my mind rested and I simply sat at my little window waiting for the breeze.

SHIRLEY, THE GIRL WHO HAD played the boy in our freshman play, joined the boarders for a while. Her father had been transferred to Houston on short notice, her parents had to find a house, her mother had to manage the move, and there was a new baby besides. Shirley thought she could have helped her mother, but she wasn't the best student in the world, and her parents didn't want her to get behind.

Sister Rose put her in the bed beside me. She was a diligent student but she had a hard time with math. We sat in the back of study hall and I helped her. She got up early to go to Mass with me every morning. One rainy Sunday afternoon we sat on the stairs outside the dormitory and found ourselves talking about faith.

The conversation began because she asked me what I thought about Saint Thérèse, the Little Flower. She was Sister Paula Thérèse's patron saint, and we heard about her a lot.

"I don't think about her at all," I said. I wanted Shirley to go first.

"Don't you think it's weird to decide that you want to be a saint? Like wanting to be a doctor or a movie star?"

"Yes."

"And going to the Pope so that she could enter the Carmelites early? What was the big deal? A year or two she couldn't be holy at home?"

I laughed. "Maybe she was afraid she would do something wrong and she wouldn't get to be a saint."

"Do you ever think about that?"

"Being a Carmelite?"

"Being a saint."

"Gosh no. Do you?"

"No. It seems proud, doesn't it? But maybe it's like anything else. If you want to accomplish it, you have to aim for it. You know, go out of your way. And in the old days, you could die for your faith. If you couldn't be a martyr, you could get sick. They didn't have antibiotics."

I smiled. I had thought Shirley was dumb! Suddenly I remembered my eighth-grade essay. Talking fast, I told Shirley all about it: my theory that Maria Goretti chose to be a martyr. It fit right in with her idea about deciding to be a saint. And I told her how the judges thought I cheated.

She said, "I guess when you get old you can't believe that kids think thoughts, too. I bet, minute for minute, we think more than they do."

I liked her a lot.

Soon we were comparing our morning experiences taking Communion. Whether we had "felt Jesus." Where we had felt him: Stomach? Chest? Both of us assumed that Communion was a physical experience that represented the spiritual and somehow verified its intensity. One day we wondered aloud if other girls felt it, too. If everyone did. We cornered another boarder and asked her. She looked at us as if we were nuts. Shirley and I laughed so hard tears came down our cheeks, and we hugged one another.

Whenever we were free, we were together. We talked the old librarian into lending us the *Spiritual Exercises* of Saint Ignatius Loyola and took turns reading it aloud to one another. We planned our own novenas, nine days of saying one hundred ejaculations a day for the poor souls in purgatory. Before confession on Saturday, we combed through the week together, trying to remember our sins. We had long conversations about what constituted a mean thought, jealousy, pride, and sloth.

With Shirley I felt I could talk about what was inside me. I told her how hard I prayed. I had begun praying in a workmanlike way, carefully thinking of each word as a stone with which I could build a road to Jesus. I tried to meditate. I stopped asking for anything for myself. I had long ago quit praying to win tournaments or make A's. What I wanted was to be made liquid, if not spirit; to lose myself in the buzz my inner chanting made, to go into the emptiness of *not asking*.

Beside me, Shirley bobbed her head. *I know what you mean.*

One Sunday afternoon in the dorm we were reading from the same book, lying on Shirley's bed. We fell asleep.

"Up! Up! Off that bed!"

Sister Rose of Lima was standing at the foot of the bed, her hands on her hips, glowering at us. I leapt up and nearly fell over, not fully awake.

She said to Shirley, "I've been speaking with Sister Ursula and she is very unhappy with your English grade. You wash your face and go down to study hall right now."

"Yes, Sister," Shirley said. She was confused, but placid.

"I'll help you," I said, but Sister grabbed my sleeve.

As soon as Shirley left, Sister set me to helping her rearrange our bed assignments. She moved me to the other end of the dorm next to the seniors. She was on a tear. She hauled out drawers and stuck them in new chests. She pulled ones out and when they were messy, she dumped them on the beds. We pulled off bedding and piled it on the beds. All through this I was crying, offended and baffled, but Sister pretended she didn't notice.

She left me in my cubicle trying to put things in order.

At supper we all had reassigned seats. I was seated with freshmen, at a different table from Shirley, who was facing away from me. In everything that we boarders did in the week that followed, Shirley and I were separated. Finally during a lunch hour, Shirley and I met in the bathroom. We both started crying. She said that Sister Rose thought that we had been developing an unnatural relationship. I could tell that it worried Shirley. She wouldn't look me in the eye. I kept saying, "A *what?* A *what?*" but Shirley didn't really know, either.

Finally she whispered fiercely, "She thinks we were doing something wrong together." I reached for her and she ran out of the room. The next weekend, her parents came from Houston to get her. Sister Rose acted as if nothing had happened. She never said a word about it. I called my mother and tried to tell her about it, but she put me off. "You exaggerate, honey," she said. "I'm sure you misunderstood." She said she would talk to Sister, but she never did.

THE NEXT SEMESTER a new boarder came, Janie Redford. She was from a small town down near Dallas, and she was being sent to boarding school because she had been sneaking around with an older boy. "They're so afraid I'll *do it*," she said. "As if I wouldn't have already if I'd wanted to."

"You didn't want to?" I asked.

"You only do it if you're going steady and he gives you his jacket." Amazed at my ignorance, she sneaked in *Seventeen* for me to read.

I helped her with her essays and algebra.

In the spring, her parents invited me for the weekend. Like a puppet on a pendulum, I swung.

Mrs. Redford picked us up. She was quite chic, with her salon hairdo and nails. Janie and I sat in the backseat and lolled on one another. Every once in a while Mrs. Redford would think of something she needed to tell Janie—bits of gossip about other town girls, or about relatives. Someone was getting married in two weeks, the world's shortest engagement, what did Janie think? and Janie nearly strangled with amusement, mouthing a word to me I couldn't get, until she mimed a bulging belly and I knew she had said "pregnant." Mrs. Redford said the wedding bans were being "pushed on through" because the bride's grandmother wasn't well and they didn't want her to die before the wedding. At that, Janie made a face and grabbed my arm.

"Ow!" I'd had my B-12 shot before we left and my arm was sore.

"You ought to get it in your butt," Janie said.

"Sister says that too, but I'm not going to pull my panties down in front of her!"

We laughed until our bellies hurt.

MR. REDFORD was a big man with a barrel chest and a bushy moustache. When supper was over, Janie and I washed and dried the dishes while he sat in his chair, tipped back, drinking a clear liquid from a jar. Janie saw me looking at it and mouthed something, but I shrugged; later she said it was moonshine, and had to explain what that was. "You really don't know anything, do you?" she said good-naturedly. She would make me her project.

Her mother called us into the living room and said she had a little surprise. She had arranged for a brunch reception in honor of Janie's guest. Ten of Janie's girlfriends were coming, most of them with their mothers. It took me a moment to understand that I was the guest. That she was having a party for me. I was speechless.

She pulled up the lid of the freezer chest to show us the food she had prepared: cheese balls, tiny éclairs, triangles of bread spread with minced ham. She handed the packages to us and we carried them to the table; from there, she transferred them to the refrigerator where they would defrost. Then she set about making pimento cheese for sandwiches, pushing yellow cheese through a grinder.

She let us take the car so Janie could drive me around and show me the school, the church, and the houses where various friends lived. Janie parked in front of one house and said it was where her "true love," Tom, lived. He was the older boy who had got her in trouble with her curfew.

"Are we going in?" I asked.

She just laughed. "He's out, you can be sure of that." She turned on the radio and the voices of the Everly Brothers blasted. We tapped our fingers on the dashboard, hummed and giggled, then drove away.

That night after her parents went to bed we used peroxide to make streaks in our hair. I fluffed my hair this way and that, studying it in the mirror. Janie set my hair with rollers and clips, plucked my eyebrows, and sawed away at what was left of my bitten nails. Then we tried on her clothes until we found something for each of us to wear.

I confessed that the thought of a deep hot bath, in which I could sit as long as I wanted, was my idea of heaven, so she found me a fluffy big towel and washcloth, some bubble bath, and a robe, and sent me into the bathroom to indulge while she lounged, catching up on magazines.

Lying back in the tub, I felt weightless and blissful.

I loosened the drain plug with my foot and enjoyed the sucking sensation as the water slowly ran out. Just before the tub was empty, I stopped the drain again and added hot water. The plastic bottle we had used for the peroxide was on the side of the tub. For no reason except a lazy, vague playfulness, I filled it with water and shook it, then squeezed as hard as I could, holding it upside down, so that the stream made the surface of the water break. I filled it again, leaned back, and pointed it at myself, spraying my neck, my chest, my shoulder. Again, and this time I raised my chin and sprayed my neck; I caught my ear with a blast that made me laugh. I filled it again, opened my legs, raised my knees, and aimed it right between my legs. I didn't think about what I was doing. One thing simply led to another. I filled the bottle, held it out as far as

I could with one hand, opened my labia with my other hand, and aimed. I felt a sensation sharp as a shock, but it was pleasant. Next, I inserted the filled bottle and squeezed. I liked the stream to hit me externally better, and after half a dozen tries I had found the exact point that felt best. With a little manipulation with my fingers, I could create the perfect bull's-eye. It made me feel something completely new; it was amazing. I didn't want to stop.

"Are you drowning in there?" Janie called from the door, and then she opened it.

I dropped the bottle to the floor and jumped.

"Oops," Janie said, scooping up the bottle.

I got out, and she handed me the towel. I was the very picture of someone caught at it, but who would think of that? Janie didn't seem to notice. She brushed her teeth while I dried myself and dressed, and then we went to her bed and talked until we fell asleep, mid-sentence.

The next morning Mrs. Redford woke us up to get dressed. She had brought huge cups of frothy hot chocolate to drink in bed. Janie said that was how Mexicans fixed it.

We found the living room transformed. Mrs. Redford had moved the furniture around, draped a long table with a snowy white damask cloth, set out a punch bowl and cups, beautiful small plates and forks. We helped her set out the food, and Janie's friends began to arrive. Everyone was dressed up, with lots of makeup. I was glad Janie had helped me apply my own. As each person entered, we were introduced. Over and over again I heard, "We're so glad you could visit us."

Soon the house was filled with laughter and chatter. Girls huddled and broke apart, hugged one another, touched arms. Their mothers were only slightly more subdued, drinking champagne and orange juice. I was still amazed that Mrs. Redford had gone to the trouble, but aware, too, that I was just an excuse for a party, that these people loved to get together. I remember thinking: *Who knew?* In years to come, I would remember that morning as someone might look back on a visit to a tropical isle; I would look back in wonder at another culture, another life, so unlike the one I lived.

I went home with Janie twice more. Once her dad drove us to a nearby town and left us at the movies, to be picked up later on. As soon as we were inside, Janie bought popcorn and a Coke, gave them to me, kissed my cheek, said, "See you, don't worry!" and was gone before I could protest.

Later she said she had arranged to meet her boyfriend—the older one—and she had tried to get him to bring someone for me, too, but he had said it wasn't a good time. "He had something special in mind," she said, atwitter. Of course she wanted me to ask what it was, but I clapped my hand over her mouth to stop her. I was embarrassed, and maybe jealous.

"I don't want to hear," I said. "It's better if I don't know." She laughed at me unkindly and flounced off to bed. The next time I was there, though, she talked about it as if she had already told me what happened. She said she wished it hadn't been in the back seat of a car. "I was so worried," she said.

"Of getting pregnant?"

"No, silly. He had a rubber." We were lying in bed. She turned on her side, whispering, "I've heard that sometimes if it's your first time, a boy's penis can get stuck, you know? And I kept thinking of that. What would we have done? Did you ever hear of that happening?"

I had not.

She sighed. "I asked him, before he put it in, if he was sure it would be okay. He said, 'Relax, why don't you?' To tell you the truth, it wasn't very romantic."

"Guess not," I said, thinking that it sounded terrible, wondering if it hurt.

"But now it's done!" she said brightly.

"Like an inoculation," I said. I wanted something better, I knew that much.

We kissed and hugged at the end of the year and swore to stay in touch.

In April 1962, I ran into Janie on the street in Austin near the university. Neither of us had known that the other was going to school there. We skipped our afternoon classes and spent the rest of the day catching up. I had no close friends. Seeing her seemed a miracle. We immediately made plans to live together in the fall, but late in the summer she called me in Wichita Falls to say that she was pregnant and was getting married. It was the boy she'd loved all along, Tom.

EARLY IN JUNE right after I had visited them and soon after I was home for the summer, Mrs. Redford called to invite me to join their family on a trip to San Miguel Allende, in Mexico, but Mother wouldn't let me go. She said she wanted me with her. She sent me down to the hospital to volunteer, but they didn't have a program. When I told Aunt Mae, who had hospital experience, she went with me and marched me to Central Supply, where she told them what I would do. I did a circuit of the nurses' stations with a supply cart, seeing what supplies they needed and providing them.

I learned to operate the autoclave. I called Rita Boosalis, too, the girl I had met in church between seventh and eighth grades. We did our usual things, swimming, talking, cooking.

As it turned out, I did get a trip after all. Daddy took Karen and me on a car trip that lasted two weeks. We went to Balmorhea springs the first night to swim, fish, and camp, and then went on to Carlsbad Caverns. We stopped at the Grand Canyon, then went on to Disneyland, San Francisco, the Great Salt Lake, Las Vegas, and home. We saw Johnny Mathis sing in Las Vegas. We saw the Hoover Dam. We floated in the Great Salt Lake.

I'm amazed that Daddy managed this trip. We had an old car and very little money. We almost never ate in a café. Instead, we carried an ice chest and lived on bologna-and-cheese sandwiches, apples and bananas, and hamburgers from little stands. We stayed in cheap motels except in Las Vegas, where we stayed at a hotel. Out by the huge swimming pool, Daddy ordered a drink for himself and Shirley Temples for Karen and me. He said it was all a bargain, because we weren't gamblers. As we headed home, he confessed that "things are pretty tight now." We piled our bags behind the front seats to extend the back seat into a sort of bed where Karen and I slept. Daddy tried to stretch his legs out in the front. We washed up in the bathrooms at service stations. We had two flats and I don't know how many times the car overheated and we sat it out on the side of the road while Daddy poured water into the radiator. For reasons I will never understand, we didn't take a camera, and I have no record of the trip, at least nothing tangible. But when I think of Daddy, and I feel that awful roiling mix of anger and sorrow, hate and love, I like to think of us on some side road as night falls, chewing day-old sandwiches and drinking water from a washed-out milk bottle, then bedding down every which way in that old car. I see myself rising up one last time to look out at the sky and the stars, then bending over the seat to kiss his neck and whisper, "Thank you."

I expect it was Mother's idea. Two weeks that she could drift. But it was Daddy who drove, who worried but didn't show it, counting his dollars when he thought I wasn't looking; it was Daddy who made sure we knew what we were seeing and that we were thrilled. We spent two nights in Las Vegas. The second night, after we had come back from the Johnny Mathis show, I was sleeping on a cot and Daddy had to scoot by me to get to the bathroom. He bumped the cot and woke me. He came out of the bathroom and stopped at the foot of my cot. There was no light on my face; he didn't know that I was awake. I could see him, though. He looked over at my sister, then at me. He brought his hand up and covered his mouth and held it there like someone who has forgotten something important and knows it is going to come back at him sooner or later.

I WENT BACK TO SCHOOL in the fall of 1959 like someone marching off on military orders. I had no enthusiasm for it but I didn't protest. Once I got there, nothing felt right. There was no Shirley to bare my soul to, no Janie to bring me *Seventeen*. There was only the same routine. I went through my days so vacantly I was called to the principal's office about my bad attitude. Some girls had complained that I was rude. One said I had criticized her play poster. I had even given Shannon's new shoes a dirty look! I had nothing to say for myself. Sister leaned close and breathed in my face: *What in heaven's name was wrong with me?* Little by little my exile became unendurable. I rose as always to attend Mass but my feet seemed too heavy to shuffle up the aisle to the Communion rail. I made B's on tests and didn't care. My debate partner complained that I didn't like her. (I did.) The only thing that felt good was to touch myself in the tub as I had at Janie Redford's house, and what was that good for but a quick shiver?

I cried in the dark. I scratched and dug at my heels until they were ragged and bleeding. With thumb and forefinger I plucked hunks from my thick eyebrows, shedding hairs on my pillow, my desk, the chapel pew.

Then one day a Persian girl came to stay with us while her parents searched for a way to reunite their scattered refugee family. The girl never stopped weeping, day or night, subsiding to whimpers only in fretful sleep. She told us in her halting English that in Iran her mother had been a ballerina and her father a writer; they had fled the terror of the despotic shah. I was fascinated yet also repulsed. I tried never to be near her, as if her anguish might infect me. At night I pulled my pillow over my head to muffle the sounds of her sobbing. One day she broke into the dormitory's locked cabinet and stole a full bottle of aspirin. That night she swallowed it with a bottle of cough syrup. She might have died if another girl had not had a hacking cough that sent Sister Rose to the broken cabinet after midnight. Dressed in her nightgown and robe, her head roughly covered by a muslin scarf, Sister Rose went up and down the aisles, bending down close to each of us, listening to the sounds of our breathing. The Persian girl's deep unnatural sleep announced itself in snorts and gargles. Sister tried to rouse her, then ran off for help. Two husky sisters returned with her and carried the girl away. The rest of us bounded from our beds and gathered to recount everything we thought we knew about the girl, wondering how we had failed to grasp the significance of her silence at lights out. At first I was like the rest of them, trembling with the thrill of someone else's calamity. Sister Rose came back and we took one another's hands impulsively, still too stunned to scatter. Sister said the girl had vomited and was pacing the corridor in the sisters' quarters; she would be okay. To our surprise, Sister did not scold us. Instead, we all traipsed down to the basement kitchen, where she made hot cocoa and admonished us to take our sorrows to the Lord. I looked around. Most of the other girls went home every weekend. They came back singing new rock-and-roll songs. Some of them had boyfriends. They chewed gum right up to the front door. They felt sorry for the Persian girl, and they would say a prayer for her at tomorrow's Mass, but she was as strange to them as an aardvark. Only I had any real idea how she felt.

Back in bed, I clasped my rosary and prayed with the terror of someone chased by hounds. I thought of my mother in her bed, asleep. What if she did not wake up? What if I never saw her again? In the morning I woke up entirely panicked, as if Mother might die by afternoon, *simply because I was not there.*

I understood the girl from Iran.

As the other boarders dressed, I went around and begged them in conspiratorial whispers to give me their allowances so I could go home, right then, that very day. I told them, *I can't stand it anymore.* They were delighted to contribute to what they saw as my daring escape. They made no connection to the previous night's excitement; they thought I was running away from the sisters. Not one girl gave me away. I left everything in my locker, and my bed unmade. I dressed in my uniform, in case a sister saw me on my way downstairs, but I carried a red cotton skirt, folded tightly, and tucked my wallet into my armpit. I crept down the stairs and changed in a parlor room near the front door. I abandoned my navy skirt folded on a piano bench and left the building without encountering anyone. I walked blocks away, glancing behind me, took a bus to town, and then got onto a long-distance bus before the sisters figured out what had happened.

What a scandal. I mortified my mother, but I had my way. The sisters shipped my possessions home in a box, C.O.D., with a terse note that they would pray for me.

SIX

I was thinking about boys. I wondered what went on inside their minds. I wondered if you could ever trust them. I saw them every day now; I sat near them in classes and brushed their shoulders coming in and out of doorways. In little flashes, I saw my hand on a boy's bicep, a squeeze around the fleshy mound, the surprise when he turned to see that it was me. All I had to do was reach out. A boy who sat in front of me in geometry got his hair cut; on his neck where it was fresh-shaven, there was a row of red pimples, small like spider bites, along the white border of skin. Sometimes, moving between desks, close to boys, I smelled hot musk rising from their shirts.

At first I had been afraid of the sear of their gazes, but soon I knew that I wasn't even in their line of sight. There were so many curvy girls who knew how to dress and what to say. The rest of us made way for them in the crowded halls, clutching books to our chests, sometimes flattening our backs to the cold, steel lockers. No one spoke to me. I was a new immigrant, ignorant of the customs.

This was really home now, Odessa. I wasn't just visiting. I was a high-school junior in public school for the first time. I had been home a week before I went up to the high school. Someone pointed down a long hall: turn here, turn there. I stopped at a classroom window and looked in. A boy caught my eye and stuck out his tongue, lapping air.

I went home without enrolling. It would take me two more tries. Finally, I took the plunge, negotiating with a counselor to assign credits for my oddball Catholic courses; I came home with a schedule. By then it was the first of December. Karen threw her arms around me. *You really have come home!* She had only a few blocks to walk to her school. As I set out each day I left her in the kitchen, packing her lunch. *Good luck,* she always said. Nearly two miles from school, I lived too close to qualify for district transportation; the school bus often passed by me as I walked the long blocks, tucking my head down like someone bent into swirling snow. Cars passed, packed with laughing students, the bass of their loud radios pounding; no one waved or thought to offer a ride. All the grooves were made already. Kids weren't mean, just vacant. There were so many of us crowded into those buildings.

I had arrived to discover that our father lived in a rented room two blocks away and one street over from our house. No one explained this to me. I asked Karen when he had moved. She said it had happened over a weekend while she was in Kermit with Aunt Mae and Uncle Howard.

"Were they fighting?" I asked. She shrugged and looked away. "They must have been fighting," I said, though they had never quarreled much.

She said, "I don't think she likes him anymore."

I tried to remember *them,* but they had disappeared while I was gone. "I think she likes Tommy," Karen whispered. Thomas Miller had been our family doctor since 1955. I opened my mouth to protest, but I had nothing to say. Karen had been here the months I was gone and I thought she was probably right. Mother was sick and needed Tommy; how could we quarrel with his presence? In the fifties, some doctors made house calls, at least some of the time; our Dr. Miller didn't even have to be called. He was like an uncle dropping by, you looked up and didn't think anything of it.

Daddy came over a few times a week. He didn't seem unhappy. He popped into Mother's bedroom for a minute or two. "Everything okay?" he'd ask us, and of course we nodded yes, swallowing our lonesomeness like dry lumps of bread. His landlady's phone number was taped on the wall by the kitchen phone. He reminded us we could call him, but we knew we wouldn't find him home. Like a fireman, he was often on call, often for sites far from Odessa. He was an oil-field hand, called a "helper"; he didn't have regular days off. His neck and arms were burnt a ruddy sienna, and through his burred hair, his scalp was purplish brown. At least it was a steady, salaried job. Maybe it didn't matter where he lived, if he was working all the time.

·

I TOLD MOTHER how scared I was, how Odessa High School had three buildings and a complicated schedule of bells, how students slumped in their classes and made obscene gestures from the back of the room. I'd learned in a week not to raise my hand, to answer only when called on, and never to seem eager. She said I was on my own. I said I had no clothes.

Aunt Mae came from Kermit with hand-me-downs from a rich girl's closet, pretty things that made me self-conscious. She took them in and she sewed me a pleated skirt; she ordered blouses from Sears. We shopped for flats and a warm jacket on sale. She bought me a bra you could inflate with a tiny straw. She said I'd done the right thing, coming home, she didn't know how Edith could stand to have me any other place. She said we could always come live with her. They were living in a crowded old Halliburton house, three rooms lined up like railroad cars. It didn't matter, there was always room. And fun. Aunt Mae was a great believer in good times. She thought we had to make our own, because good times didn't come looking for you. If all we could think of was jumping rope and baking a cake, it was better than sulking, she said. I knew what she was about. The great distracter, she was, and a lot of the time, she saved the day, knowing all the while a time was coming bigger than all of us.

In her room, Mother lay with a pillow over her head, the blinds drawn, waiting for dark, for her pills, for her doctor. I'd imagined her gratitude and some kind of recovery, but there were days she staggered and slurred her words, knocked over water glasses, and could not be trusted with a cup of tea. Her hair was dingy. She wept until her pillow was soaked (but she did not complain). On better days she seemed to be absorbed in listening to something we couldn't hear; she slept a lot. My sister, at twelve, took care of herself. She had been living on canned soup and peanut-butter sandwiches. To that I added scrambled eggs, macaroni and cheese, a wider selection of canned goods, when I bothered. She washed her clothes and hung them on the backs of chairs in the kitchen. She ironed her skirts and her dresses with bows in the back. At night she sat at the table, her brow furrowed, her head bent low over her homework: arithmetic problems and assigned essays ("themes") about states of the union. Her pencil had made a callus on her finger. Now she asked me to check her work, everything neat, cramped. Even if I said it was perfect, she copied it over one last time. I moved her out of her bed and took it for my own. She slept in a room off the kitchen in the front corner of the house. I said I had to listen for Mother. I said I stayed up late. After boarding school, I relished privacy.

In the evenings we tiptoed in to tell Mother goodnight. Sometimes she patted the bed and we sat with her until her eyelids fluttered. I spied her rosary on her dresser and put it under her pillow.

Later, after Karen was in bed, Mother got up to wash and change her gown. You could see her gather her strength for the effort. I was worried she would fall and I got in the habit of going into the bathroom with her. I ran the water to the perfect temperature. I washed her hair. I gently scrubbed her back. If she had had a bad day she didn't get in the tub. Instead, she sat on a folded towel on the toilet seat and I washed her with a cloth and dried her. If she felt better, we chatted, none of it mattering much. She began to ask me about school, and I tried to find interesting things to say, or at least positive things. I straightened her bed, tucking the sheets and fluffing her pillows, folding back the spread. She liked to sit up on top of the covers. Then the doctor came, usually between ten and eleven. She was his last stop each night. He entered through a door to her bedroom directly off the porch. Sometimes I jumped up from the bed. Sometimes I was standing in the hall. Sometimes he tried to engage me: How was school? How was I feeling? I went out and shut the door.

She seemed to light up when he arrived, no matter how bad she was feeling. She touched her hair. She reached out her hand to him, palm up, a curious gesture. It was perfectly clear why Daddy had moved. Where would he have slept, coming home in the middle of the night? I was torn between loyalty to him and gladness at anything that made Mother feel better, even this kind old balding doctor. Middle ground was my coolness.

"At least you could be polite," Mother said. "Tommy could change your future," an absurd thing to say. *Dr. Miller,* I wanted her to call him *Dr. Miller,* to put him in his place. That was an absurd idea, too, of course, and I knew it.

Daddy called him Tommy. Everyone did. He was gentle and thorough and patient. He explained things. And Mother depended on him. He had learned all the things that pained her. First her body, then her heart. I remember so clearly how he would sit in her high-back chair in the bedroom. Sometimes he smoked a cigarette or even had a drink. The door to the bedroom would be open and I'd come and go in the hall and see him, a little slumped with weariness. It was as if he caught his breath before he went home, as if Mother's bedroom were a *salon.* She would be speaking in a soft voice and he would smile or shake his head. He talked to her about hospital politics and the state of the nation. He brought her last month's magazines from his office waiting room. She craved these small connections to the outside world. His company.

I always thought I minded on Daddy's behalf, but I realize now that I was jealous that Tommy could comfort and amuse her best, instead of me.

Karen asked me, "When will she get better?"

I told her she should ask Dr. Miller, so she did. She crouched in the hallway between Mother's door and the bathroom and waited for him to arrive. She heard him on the porch and ran to signal me. We went into the bedroom and sat by Mother, one on each side. "Well, well," he said. "Everyone's here!" He cupped his palm gently against Karen's cheek.

"I want someone to tell me what's going on," she said prissily. "I'm not a baby."

"You shouldn't worry," he said. "That's my job."

"I'm sorry," Mother said. I supposed she was speaking to him. He told us we should go to bed. It was getting late. Karen, in a rare show of temper, stomped out of the room.

I followed her to her bed. I told her that Mother loved us but was too sick to show it. *I know that,* she said. *That's not what I asked.* The truth was, I didn't understand what was wrong with Mother. I had to pay more attention. I had to learn to ask questions. I knew that she was hurting, that she was weak. Why else would she be in bed, where she had no life unless she dreamed it?

I sat on the edge of the bed and studied my sister. Her eyes were narrowed with anger and frustration. Her pale blond hair was chopped off short. She sat with her knees pulled up to her chin and I saw that her panties were frayed. She never asked for anything. But that night she said she didn't see why she couldn't sleep in the other twin bed beside me, and I said, *For heavens' sake, grow up. Why don't you go to Kermit?* I asked her. Aunt Mae and Uncle Howard were going to move to Monahans soon, to a new house, a "real" house, with a shower and central cooling. They said both of us could come. Our cousin Joan's room would have twin beds, one for Karen. I wanted her to go. I didn't know how to help her, I didn't know how to be a sister. I stood up and gave her a dismissive look.

She was stubborn, jutting her jaw out to make a point.

She's my mother, too.

RITA BOOSALIS was my only friend. She saw me in the halls at school: *I can't believe it! Why didn't you call?* We had different classes, so we talked at night on the phone until her mother made her hang up. I started spending Saturday nights with her, then coming home after Mass. At first I complained about school, but she wanted to talk about boys. We lay in bed whispering until we fell asleep. She didn't have any experience, either, but she had a running file on a dozen boys. She knew whom they had dated and for how long. None of them were the going-steady type—good news, if you thought about it. She knew what cars they drove. She had heard who were the good kissers, who tried to push their luck. Once Billy Vandermeer, who lived just around the corner from Rita, had given her a ride home, and the glove compartment fell open and there was a big jar of Vaseline jelly. Disgust and glee contorted her face as she told me. It didn't mean a thing to me; I had to bear her astonished gaping at my ignorance. (This was from a girl who had baby words for going to the bathroom.) I wanted to know who was smart, but all the boys in honors classes were geeks, she said. So were the boys in Catholic Youth. We talked about going to their events anyway but never did. If word got around that you were Catholic, you were stuck.

Ultimately, the most satisfying topics were speculative. We were each waiting for someone to come over the horizon. He would be cute, smart enough, a good dancer, polite, easy with parents, a good kisser (not too much spit). I thought the tennis players (skinny, quickstepping, not too full of themselves) were cute; I'd studied last year's yearbook. Rita longed for a boyfriend who played football. She loved the team jackets, and how the players' girls wore them running onto the field at the end of the game. What I wanted was a boy who talked to you and not about you to his buddies. Rita said it was up to you to make him respect you. If that ran him off, he wasn't the one. She hadn't ever actually dated. Her parents had only let her go to group events, fortunately including the youth center, where at least she could check things out. We practiced dancing, then went together, dopey on the sidelines, trying to look eager, for all the good it did. She got to dance and I did not. Sometimes she disappeared for fifteen minutes. Whatever she knew about kissing, I was sure she had learned it there in the shadows near the toilets, or outside around the corner of the building. She would turn seventeen in March, the magic number that would allow her to date. She had someone in mind.

I can just see us now, making key-lime pie (sweet evaporated milk, raw eggs, lemon juice, no lime at all) and listening to Top 40 on the radio at her house while we projected our fantasies onto the screen of future opportunity. Her parents were Cajun Catholics from Louisiana (*Looziana*), and she'd had plenty drilled into her about Our Lady of Virtue. She had a full bosom and hips and beautiful coppery skin and black hair, but she was poor, like me, and short. She would never look like one of those sweater twin-set types from the side of town that had trees. In daylight, she was full of admonitions. She told the story of her parents' courtship:

Catholic virgins both, a year's engagement, and no hanky panky until the wedding night. She told me often that purity was a treasure, but I knew that at night she sank into dreamy dreams I had not yet had; I thought they might arrive with menstruation. Sometimes she trembled like a dozing puppy. She liked to talk about the delight her husband would express when he discovered she was a virgin. She said we had to guard our virtue, that same old story. I didn't think she needed to worry.

MOTHER WAS HURTING, hardly able to stand up. The pain medicine made her clumsy but it didn't do the trick. Her buttocks were splotched purple from injections. Her nails were chewed to the quick. Her hair smelled sour.

"It's too much," she moaned. "It isn't fair. It isn't fair!"

It was the week before Christmas. Tommy Miller said, "We'd like to keep an eye on her. We'll make her comfortable." I was starting to think of him as *Tommy*. It helped so much when he was there. You knew he would make her feel better. She felt better as soon as she heard his car pull into the drive.

I called Daddy's landlady. He was in the field.

Mother went to the hospital in a cab, trying to look brave. From the back seat as she drove away she waved her hand back and forth like a window washer. We waved back like watchers at the end of a parade. Karen sidled near me, and I took her hand to walk back in the house.

Later, Daddy went up to the hospital, then came to the house with a bag of hamburgers. Karen and I set upon the food like refugees. He told us, "She's had a spell." He didn't seem concerned.

My grandmother came from Wichita Falls to help out. She had brought Mother a pretty chenille robe, rosy red, and flannel pajamas for Karen and me. She was used to coming on short notice; Mother had always had a fragile constitution. She's the one who finally told me that the trouble with Mother's kidneys was chronic and had a name, Bright's disease. When I heard that, I thought, *What a terrible thing to call a sickness!* Besides that, her migraines were bad again, and she was a funny color from recurring hepatitis, things you never got over. The hair on her head was thinning, too.

With Mother in the hospital, there wasn't anything for my grandmother to do, but doing wasn't the point, being there was. She stayed at the hospital overnight, then came home part of the day to sleep and make supper for us. We had real meals, with meat, potatoes, a vegetable. Aunt Mae came and took Karen back to Kermit for the holidays.

My grandmother had brought a television from Wichita Falls. She said Mother had written, complaining of boredom. I watched it alone each night until the last program was over. The station tested the emergency frequency, played the national anthem, then died. I went to bed with chocolate bars or potato chips, and read until I couldn't keep my eyes open. *All Quiet on the Western Front. Jude the Obscure. Roan Stallion,* a shocking narrative poem by Robinson Jeffers. I went to the library and these dark books had the pull of a magnetic field. After years of saints' lives, I craved sin. I craved pain and death on the page so I could cry, then close the book and turn off the light. I seldom said a standard prayer. Instead, I squeezed my eyes shut so hard I saw stars and I raised my face heavenward. I thought there were prayers inside me that had no words and God would know what they were even if I did not. Once, overcome with an impulse like the one I had had in boarding school, I lay on the wood floor, face down, my arms stretched out, and I felt a burning in my throat like a coal on fire. I never stopped to think that I had eaten chili for supper; I thought God had finally heard me crying out.

. . .

Mother came home on Christmas and the next day Aunt Mae brought the kids over. Karen and our cousin Joan were wearing mouton fur jackets and red corduroy pants. The baby, Judy, had a doll half as big as she was. Mike, two years younger than the big girls, had stayed with Uncle Howard; they would come later. We would have a second Christmas, here, with Mother. Aunt Mae had brought a ham and my grandmother made a coconut cake and two kinds of pie. She cooked all morning, using a cloth to dab at her eyes. She looked grim and determined. She saw me watching her. "Flour," she said, swiping the air in front of her face.

Daddy showed up mid-morning and then Tommy came by. He said he had just a few minutes. My grandmother had bought a carton of eggnog, and he drank some from a coffee cup, then said he had something for me in the car. It was a big electric typewriter from his office. Daddy carried it in. "Will you look at that," he said. Tommy had tied a red ribbon around it. He laughed and said, "I hope you don't mind, it's from the office, used." Then he went home. Aunt Mae said I could have showed a little more appreciation.

Mother called us into her room. She said we might as well do our gifts now. There were paper dolls for Joan, barrettes for Judy. She sent me to her dresser to pull out two wrapped boxes for

Karen and me. Karen's held a pearl drop necklace, and mine was a silver charm bracelet. I wondered who had shopped for it. Daddy gave me five dollars and a slide rule. He gave Karen her own fishing pole. He had a package of Whitman's chocolates for us all to share. He handed it to my grandmother, who looked startled, then passed it on to Joan. Mother said she was going back to bed until dinner, and Daddy said he had an errand to run. My grandmother and Aunt Mae went back to the kitchen, and the little kids went outdoors. I stayed with Mother until it was just the two of us, then gave her a kiss. She hardly noticed, sliding down under the sheet, putting her arm over her eyes.

I went into the bathroom to take an inventory of my looks for about the hundredth time since I had come home. I plucked my thick eyebrows and made a nice arch. I thought of all the times I had watched my mother draw on her own eyebrows, glancing back and forth at me while she chatted, offering me beauty secrets. She advised me always to choose clothes in colors that played up my eyes, as if I bought a new wardrobe every season, like the daughters of oilmen and bankers, surgeons and senators, the kind of men I knew she thought she should have married but had not known in time.

Using the little scissors from the medicine chest, I hacked at my hair until I had bangs. Then I ran a bath and washed my hair, lying back in the hot water until it covered all of me but the tip of my nose and my bent legs.

THE GOOD SMELLS of cooking wafted through the house. Mother got up and found me reading on my bed.

"They're a little short, pumpkin," she said.

I blushed and tugged at my bangs.

"Of course they'll grow," she said. I would never be as pretty as my mother wanted me to be, which was as pretty as she once was.

She was wearing a ratty quilted nylon robe that hung to just below her knees. I started to ask her why she didn't wear the pretty chenille robe my grandmother had given her, but I lost my nerve. She had pulled on a pair of Daddy's boot socks, tugging them up as high as they would go, leaving bands of pale skin between socks and robe. I followed her into the kitchen. There was a booth in the corner of the room with red vinyl cushions like you see in cafés, and Aunt Mae and my grandmother were sitting there across from one another, their coffee cups on the table before them. My grandmother said, "There you are, my precious," looking at my mother; it was an expression she had used toward me countless times. Aunt Mae scooted over as Mother slid in. My grandmother got up and poured coffee for her.

I made tea and took my cup to the booth. I sat down and pressed my fingers against my temples where the throb of a migraine was suddenly sharp, the kind of pain I knew would get worse before it went away. Not now, I pleaded deep inside, the way I knew my mother must sometimes pray for a pause in her suffering. She caught my eye and smiled.

MY GRANDMOTHER had prepared a feast: baked ham, candied sweet potatoes, biscuits, and black-eyed peas. The little girls were in the kitchen booth. I sat next to Daddy at the dining table, a mistake that left us nowhere safe to look. My grandmother always pretended he didn't exist. She kept her gaze fixed on her plate. Her mouth was pursed so tight I didn't see how she could eat. Mother slouched at one end of the table, toying with her food, looking limp and bored. Aunt Mae, seated at the other end, kept jumping up and down to carry a dish in or out, or to check on the girls.

She was petulant about Uncle Howard, who was supposed to have brought Mike over for dinner. "Where is that man? Why am I always saying, 'Where is that man?' " She hadn't said a word about him coming until we sat down to eat. I thought she was just trying to fill up the air with talk instead of tension. Uncle Howard never came to Odessa. The only family gatherings he went to were at his mother's in Wichita Falls each summer. When he wasn't working, he liked to be home with his shoes off and his teeth out. My grandmother shook her head, a tiny gesture of contempt for the vagaries of men.

Nobody looked at anyone else.

Beside me, Daddy chewed methodically. He speared a slice of ham with his fork and rubbed it in the sticky juice on the platter. He was the only person who actually ate a full meal. My head was pounding and a hot dread was gurgling in my gut. Aunt Mae offered me dessert, but I said I was too full. Eating, better than talking, went on too long. My grandmother stood up.

Karen came in and hung on Daddy's shoulder. She had a round, sweet face and her hair was almost white. Her expression was solemn and benign, too old. Behind her glasses, her blue eyes seemed washed away. She had Mother's coloring and Daddy's sturdy build. We couldn't have looked more different. She seemed bathed in light—it was the migraine aura that sometimes gave me eerily distorted perceptions—and I thought, *I wonder what she's thinking.* I don't suppose it had ever before occurred to me that my little sister had thoughts of her own.

Daddy said, "Find the Chinese Checkers, Butchie, we'll play a game and then I've got to go," and as Karen hopped away, she was just a little girl again. She hated that old nickname, but Daddy didn't seem to have any idea.

My grandmother was already up, clearing the table, ignoring Daddy's plate. Aunt Mae took it and he thanked her. He called out to my grandmother, "Great meal, Frieda!" He told Mother it was nice to see her up and she gave him a wan smile.

He had made divinity the day before Christmas Eve and now he retrieved a dish of it from the cabinet on the porch and brought it to the table. He held it out toward my mother, but she shook her head. Karen found the Chinese Checkers box and set it on the table in front of him. She took a piece of candy and gave one to Joan. My grandmother brought a damp dishrag in. Daddy offered her candy, and she said, "No thanks," gruffly, and slung the cloth down beside the dish. Daddy slid it across the table away from him. Mother picked the rag up and made a couple of swipes in front of her and then tossed it away. It went off the table onto a chair. If I knew anything, that rag would be on the chair for weeks. Judy came up to Mother and she scooted the chair back and took her on her lap. Daddy asked me if I was going to play and I said I didn't think so. He held the dish up to me and I shook my head. "Well, all the more for us," he said, patting the girls on their backs. He asked them what color marbles they wanted and said he was going to beat their pants off. I had a vague idea that what had happened in the last two or three minutes was some kind of illustration of where we all stood with one another, but I shook the thought away—-too complicated, too fraught with anxiety.

I went into the bathroom and opened the vanity cupboard. The shelves were crowded with medicine bottles. I opened them and looked at the pills, ignoring the labels. I swallowed a little white pill with a handful of water, a capsule that looked familiar, and then one more for good measure. The second capsule felt stuck in my throat. I leaned over the bowl and cupped more water into my mouth. I didn't know what the pills were for. I didn't care. For about half a minute I imagined myself taking all of them, but I shook away the thought. I had tried that when I was in sixth grade, after the tornado, but I had thrown up right away. When Mother asked me, *Why, why, why,* I said I didn't know. I really hadn't known, except that for a little while I hadn't wanted to be in my life, and I was curious. I had more sense than that now.

I sat down on the edge of the tub and waited while things got sorted out in the rest of the house. I heard my mother going down to her room. She didn't shut her door. In the kitchen, my grandmother and aunt would be doing dishes. Daddy and the girls were playing. I heard Joan laughing. Chinese Checkers was our favorite game. I loved the pale green marbles. My mother had told me they were the color of certain ancient Chinese vases.

I studied my face in the mirror. Dots of light danced across my reflection. My eyes played tricks on me sometimes; it was part of the migraine. I thought maybe someday I would go blind. It would be horrible, worse than dying. I was reading my way through Erich Maria Remarque. I was on to *The Citadel*. The print was tiny, the vocabulary challenging. I liked that I had to pay close attention.

My face crumpled and I started to cry. The headache was turning me into a baby. I grabbed a towel and wiped my face hard. I looked in the mirror again and pulled myself straight. I pressed my bangs with the heel of my hand, trying to make them lie flat. What had I been thinking?

As I left the bathroom I heard Mother on the phone extension in the bedroom. "When can you come? I'm feeling shaky." I heard her hang up the phone. I waited a moment and went in. "What!" she said sharply.

"Nothing," I said. Now, instead of lights, there were holes of blackness in my vision. Parts of her face were missing. "Nothing, Mother." I was scared, but there was no one to tell. Everyone needed me to be strong so that they could look after the children and my mother and their jobs. All I really had to do was look after myself. That had been true for a long time, but in boarding school I had had only to do what was "right," and I had always known what that was because someone else defined it.

I followed the quiet sounds of my aunt and grandmother talking in the kitchen. They were in the booth, drinking coffee. Through the kitchen door I could see Judy up on my grandmother's bed. I had the sudden longing to remember being her age. It seemed unfair that you forgot the happiest part of your life.

There was a fresh uncut pie on the counter, the meringue tall and golden. I went back into the other room where Daddy and Joan and Karen were hunched over the checkerboard. Suddenly, the room spun around me. I cried out, "I'm going to be sick!" and ran for the bathroom. Behind me, Daddy knocked his chair down getting up.

I vomited violently, making a terrible mess. "Oh my nose!" I cried; it stung so much, it was so nasty.

Daddy came in and wet a washrag and wiped my face. He used a damp corner to dab gently at my nostrils. He turned on the faucet again. "Here, wash out your mouth," he said, but I had to throw up again.

I leaned over the toilet. "Sorry, sorry."

He washed out the cloth and wiped my face again. "Now, now," he said. "There can't be more. You'll be okay. Shh."

Mother was there, too. She stood at the door of the bathroom. Her arms were braced along the wood as if she was holding up the doorjamb.

Daddy said, "Go back to bed, Edith, I've got it." He was on his knees, wiping the floor and the side of the tub and toilet.

I washed out my mouth and sat down on the toilet lid. "Tough luck," he said. He balled up the dirty cloth and threw it in the corner of the room. Then he patted my forehead and declared it not too hot. He took a fresh cloth from the stack on the hamper, wet it and wiped my face again. Then he walked me out of the bathroom to my room.

"You get in bed now," he said. He went into the bathroom again and shut the door. I put on my gown. In the dimness of the bedroom, my spotted vision was less frightening. I remembered being told that as a little girl with the measles, I had been blind for a day and then I had recovered. It did not seem possible that I could forget something like that, but recently it had occurred to me that the memory of pain and fear did not necessarily stay with you forever. So in its strange way, the story of my episode of blindness comforted me, now and at other times.

My grandmother had come into the hall, too. She probably thought it was my mother who had been sick. I heard her say, "You go on to bed, sweetheart. I'll take care of her." As if Daddy had not already done so.

"Of course you'll be the one to take care of her," my mother said loudly. "That's just what you want, isn't it?"

"You don't know what you're saying," my grandmother said.

"Don't I?"

"All right," my grandmother said. I knew what she meant, saying that; that she was going to leave, that she wouldn't argue, that

Mother would have her way, that this was how it always went, a quarrel in perpetual motion.

Aunt Mae would go home and Daddy would go back to his room or wherever it was he went when he pretended he had to go. I didn't want my grandmother to leave me too. Couldn't they see that I was just a kid? Why were they angry now? I was sick. That was all that had happened. I wished they would all take care of me for a change: Daddy and Mother on one side of my bed, my grandmother and Aunt Mae on the other, all of them patting my shoulders, saying soothing things. Just this one time. They would think I was in a coma, but I would just be resting. They would all get along for my sake.

When I think of being a little girl, it always ends that day, a blip of fool's innocence all out of place in my fifteenth year, the day after Christmas 1958; that was the last time I thought the people I loved could rescue me from anything.

·SEVEN·

After her brief, last hospitalization—she died in her own bed— Mother had a kind of false spring. They had given her antibiotics and IV feedings, and she started feeling better for a short while. She got some pink color back in her cheeks and she took fewer of the drugs that made her woozy.

One morning she said, "Look in the driveway!" There was a boxy, powder-blue car, an Edsel. It was a gift from Tommy. He had bought the Edsel for his wife, who preferred a Cadillac of her own. Mother didn't mind. The car was a vote for recovery, an optimistic gesture. She would drive it into the future! So we pretended for a little while. It sat in the driveway, proof of something deserved and delivered, though nothing like what I wished for (for her, for me).

HER STIFF YELLOW HAIR showed two inches of roots. "I'll do it for you," I said. Usually she just used peroxide, but we were flush. There'd been Christmas money, too, from Tommy.

We used Lady Clairol. For me there was a strawberry blond shade. For good measure, I restyled my bangs, cutting deeper into the crown so that they sat on my head like an upside-down dish. All afternoon we giggled like kids. Karen, naturally white-haired like Mother used to be, stuck around but kept her distance, ostensibly reading a book but never turning the page.

That night I was up late with Mother after Tommy had come and gone. In a few weeks was semester change and I was going into a speech class and into honors English. My chemistry teacher, Mrs. Filleman, took a personal interest and pressed for a better schedule for me. She said the other chem class had fewer idiots. She was old, grouchy, smart, and she cared a lot. She couldn't understand why I didn't want to be a scientist. I liked her, even though I didn't like chemistry. And I was excited about the changes in my classes.

Mother ventured to ask about the boys in my classes and I heard myself describing James, in my English class, who was beautiful as a sculpture, sweet, and a quarterback besides. I couldn't believe I mentioned him. He went steady with a rich, popular girl. Mother said you can't help liking the ones you like, but it didn't sound as if I ought to get my heart in a stir. Wasn't there someone more likely, someone interesting, and conveniently unattached?

I thought of a boy in Mrs. Filleman's class. She'd have said he was one of the idiots. She was snappish with him, but he never seemed to mind. He was a senior; I heard Mrs. Filleman telling him he had better shape up or even Baylor wouldn't have him. Baptists went to Baylor; I hadn't heard that it was hard to get in. His name was Larry Predmore. His partner was a wild-haired boy who modeled himself after the singer Jerry Lee Lewis. Recently, he was missing from class, and so was my partner. Mrs. Filleman put Larry and me together. "This is purely temporary," she said.

When she was out of earshot, Larry said, "Maybe you can pull me up in here." He grinned. "If I don't pull you down."

I repeated this to Mother. She wanted more. "It means something when you remember what somebody said." She had put her book down, *Anthony Adverse*.

"He's cute, but I don't know anything about him. I don't know why I brought him up."

"Take a closer look tomorrow." She ran her hand down my silky pink-blond hair and buried her nose in the nest of my circle bangs. And I set out to bring her game, like my cat brings a bird to the back door.

He smelled pleasantly of soap and aftershave. He was nice looking and soft-spoken. He had long, graceful fingers, and a conservative haircut—no "tail," no "burr," no grease. He already looked like a man, with a square jaw and a lanky broad-shouldered build, but his slightly cocky grin was a kid's. He was relaxed, like my Uncle Howard. Now we would call him *laid back*. Maybe that was why I liked him, why Mrs. Filleman didn't.

I lay in bed and took inventory of what I knew about him. His blue eyes, a pale mole on one cheek, a cowlick at his part just before it disappeared into the hair he combed down the back of his head. He was on the early schedule, 7:30 to 2:00; I came 9 to 4.

The next day his partner was back from detention ("juvey")

and I worked alone. Larry said hello, friendly as anything, but where would that get me? I kept stealing glances at him all through class. He did everything with ease, even if he did it wrong. And he was cute.

We were coming up on finals and I knew the class was hard for him. I caught him outside the door and said maybe we could study together. I handed him a piece of paper with my phone number on it.

He looked puzzled, examined the paper, then smiled. "I never have gone out with a really smart girl before." He gave me a soft punch on the bicep.

All afternoon I was distracted, going over and over our exchange. I wasn't sure what he meant, whether it was good or bad; I didn't want to be a smart girl. I wanted to be somebody's sweetheart.

He didn't make me wait. He called at seven on the dot and the first thing he said was, "That didn't sound right, about you being smart. I'm glad you're smart, I admire it. I've thought about asking you out, but I thought maybe you wouldn't date somebody like me. I'm a pretty ordinary guy, but I think we could have fun. Only I don't want to study chemistry. I don't want to think about chemistry at all."

"Deal," I said. I went to tell my mother that I had a date with the boy from chem lab. She said, "See, I told you." She hadn't told me anything, but maybe she had meant to. Both of us broke into crazy grins.

She sat on my bed while we laid out clothes to see what I could wear. There was a new skirt, blouses, and I had Tommy to thank.

I started to worry. "I don't know why he asked me out. Maybe

he thinks I'm altogether different from what I am." I couldn't confess how I had manipulated him.

"Maybe he liked your new hair." She lay back on her pillows,
admiring me.

·

THERE WERE ONLY a few things to do on a date, but they were
new to me. I loved getting ready. I put together outfits and ran in
to see what Mother thought. I took some hems up, let others
down. She tugged and adjusted and picked off lint. She gave me
money to buy mascara and new lipstick. Larry always compli-
mented me first thing.

Aunt Mae came over and brought me a cashmere cardigan,
worn once or twice by a friend's daughter.

Friday nights, Larry and I usually went to the teen center. He
was a terrific dancer and I caught on easily. I imagined how we
looked to other kids, how even if I didn't have other friends I no
longer qualified for the derision or pity of my peers. I loved dancing, fast or slow. I got lost in it.

The last dance was always romantic and I anticipated his suggestion that we go somewhere to park. Maybe he would say, "Want
to take a drive?" Rita had said I shouldn't agree to go past the city
limits. Girls who did that went all the way in more ways than one,
even if, sometimes, they didn't really want to. We could park by
the football field, or at the construction site of the new high
school, Permian—places everyone knew. There would be other
couples in other cars, and the sense of someone nearby was like a
phantom chaperone. Sometimes a police car might drive slowly by,
but if things were quiet, the cops never bothered anyone. I wasn't

sure how Larry and I would negotiate where to go or what to do. I didn't seek any more advice from Rita, whose experience I never questioned but doubted; I wanted to find out things for myself. She had gone to junior high with Larry, and she pronounced him okay, though he had always had a smart-aleck mouth. In the end, I knew it was instinct that had made me pick him out, a lucky, almost uncanny match of temperament, more important by far than intellect. And he wasn't dumb. (Eventually he did go to Baylor and then to law school.) He could be wry, sly, ironic. He picked up on hints. My rebelliousness bubbled up; he was an energetic opponent, arguing about pop songs or movies for the fun of it. And he was sexy, in a warm, mature way, easygoing and not pushy, but presumptive. He smelled good, too.

Coming out of the center the first time, he offered me a mint. My heart did a little dance. We didn't go anywhere to park except home. We sat in the car at the curb, my introduction to necking without fear. After a few dates he started coming into the house for a while. We watched television while I sat on his lap. Sometimes Karen watched with us. She liked Larry a lot because he didn't treat her like a baby. If she was feeling up to it, Mother came in for a while. They liked one another, I could see that right away.

Saturday nights we went to a movie or a basketball game. He said he liked to play pickup games but wasn't keen enough for varsity. He explained the game to me. Later we went to the hamburger stand where everyone went to be seen. He drove around twice to check who was there and then parked. We talked. He asked where I had moved from, so I told him about boarding school. He seemed fascinated by my religion and my years in convent school. He asked the same dumb questions I'd heard before: Do nuns really shave their heads? Is there really a tunnel from the convent to the priest's house? Did I really think Protestants wouldn't get into heaven? And what the heck is Limbo? The first time he asked me, I answered each question seriously. The second time, I laughed it off. The third time he brought up nuns, he was smirking, and I said haughtily that it was time to go home. "Catholic girls don't stay out late." He laughed at me and said I was turning out to be a sensitive type. When he drove up to the house and turned off the ignition, I said, "Don't bother," and got out abruptly. That was our first quarrel.

Hot with anger, I told Mother everything. *He was sarcastic! He wouldn't let up! He thinks Baptists are better than Catholics!* Serious and sympathetic, she said you couldn't expect teenage boys to be tactful; they took longer than girls to grow up. Men were insensitive, it was their nature. They didn't know what hurt you until you taught them. And Larry was a kidder. He thought he was funny. Most of the time, he *was* funny. He hadn't meant to criticize, Mother said. Catholics were exotic in Odessa, but he hadn't wanted to let on how interesting he thought my religion was, so he had made light of it. He had misjudged what was funny and then didn't know how to back off. Boys were clumsy, and sometimes dumb as posts, and awfully proud. I had handled it just fine, and she was sure he'd learned his lesson. She gave me a kiss on the end of my nose. "It's a rocky road ahead, my pumpkin, but you will learn to tread it."

I felt better. She understood perfectly. And as if to prove her point, Larry called while we were still discussing him. She answered the phone and handed it to me with a triumphant look. He was sorry. With great effort, I resisted my urge to say he ought to be, and settled it with, "Okay." Mother was waving her hands about; obviously she wanted me to smooth things over better than that. Reluctantly, and then with relief, I said, "I probably overreacted, Larry. Let's forget it." He didn't bring up Catholic doctrine or Catholic school to me anymore. On our next date, we both acted as if our squabble had never happened. Mother pointed out that it was good to weather a little storm and see that our sails held. I thought she was right, and furthermore, I thought his apology meant that I had some kind of upper hand. I didn't realize that I was like someone always looking over her shoulder, watching for the devil to catch up. I did not understand that the true catastrophe ahead was what made everything else seem pernicious. At the center of things, I saw Larry and me as combatants, as I saw almost everyone. The better I got to know him, the more faults I found. He was a clown and the jokes were at my expense.

I didn't know how to be his girlfriend or anyone's friend, but at least it took two months for us to figure that out. And he did teach me to drive.

IN HONORS ENGLISH, I felt alive. The teacher, Miss Gorman, was an old maid with a passion for literature. She told us she had a master's degree from Columbia University in New York City, the most exciting city in the world. I told another girl that I didn't understand why Miss Gorman had come back to Texas, but the girl had heard she had nursed her mother for years and by then she was an old maid. That seemed heroic to me.

There were only fifteen of us, and though I knew none of the students outside of class, they were bright and courteous and I was comfortable with them. Miss Gorman challenged us and made us love talking about what we read. She gave us assignments to extend the lives of characters from stories and declared to me privately that she had never seen better than mine. She encouraged my writing. She gave me a copy of *Seventeen,* with the year's fiction-contest winner. She said she knew I was better, but when I showed her a story I wrote about a boy who falls in love with his girlfriend's invalid mother she said she thought it was too mature a theme for a teen magazine. That was when I told her about my mother's illness. She started sending novels home with me for Mother, and gave me her home phone number, in case I ever needed help in the middle of the night. I didn't know what to make of her. She was plain and prim and as old as my grandmother, but she talked to us like real people, and I believed her when she said our minds were precious to her, and teaching was a life's calling. All of us made A's.

I told Mrs. Everson, the speech teacher, about my debating experience, apologetic that I'd competed only against other parochial-school students. She laughed and said she was glad her students didn't have to meet up with any Jesuits, who were bound to be better for working so hard and having God on their side. I was surprised that she knew about Catholic orders, though she probably had never heard of mine. She was an obese woman, with milky-smooth skin and an exaggerated enunciation, like Bette Davis's, and she was passionate about her team. She was serious and efficient and kind. I was switched to her advanced forensics class, where students were preparing for tournaments. When I told her that my mother wasn't well and I didn't know when I could go out of town, and I didn't think I should debate, because someone would depend on me, she said I should go ahead and prepare for an individual event, and she would put my name in and I could go on short notice. There was a small fee to enroll, but the school paid it. Every day I spent the class hour reading news-magazines and writing summaries of articles, so I could do extem-poraneous speaking, an event that required on-the-spot speeches about current events. For two periods a day, I was happy. Later in the year, I started helping some of the debaters work on their briefs. Once I mentioned some of my topics to Mother, but when I realized that she didn't know what I was talking about and that I was embarrassing her, I found a way to turn the conversation to a question about the way I gestured when making a certain point, and she was able to make suggestions. After that, I brought poems to her, things I wrote at home, things that required no updates on the life of the nation.

Though I thought I'd mind not being in class with Larry, it was actually better not to have the distraction. Chemistry was hard as it was. I liked my lab partner, a girl who said she loved science bet-ter than anything. She wanted to discover new medicines. She had her whole education planned out. I assumed my growing mound of poems and stories (or, mostly, story starts) would fail to impress her, so I never mentioned my writing. I think we could have been friends if one of us had overcome our shyness, if I had not been intimidated by her math and science talents.

LARRY CALLED ALMOST EVERY NIGHT. I liked sitting on the floor with the phone cord twirled in my hand. Sometimes Mother peeked in and saw me and gave me a little wave like a moth-er in a movie. I always called Rita as soon as Larry and I were off the line. She wanted blow-by-blow accounts of our dates: everyone we'd seen, what the other girls wore, how long we sat in the car in front of the house. She said she missed my spending the night but it was great that I had Larry now. I failed to recognize her generosity.

One afternoon I came home from school and his car was parked in front of the house. I ran up the sidewalk into the house, calling "Hey you!" to an empty room. I heard his voice and Mother's laughter. I went into her room. He was sitting on the bed and they were playing cards. The bed was neatly made; even the pillows were prim under the chenille bedspread. Mother was dressed in a skirt and untucked blouse.

"Hey you," I said again, unable to hide my surprise.

"Sweetheart," my mother said.

I sat down on the bed across from Larry. The curtains were pulled back and the dusty slats of the blinds tipped to let in sun. His brown hair looked sandy in the light.

I said, "I might go to San Angelo with the speech team in two weeks," and my mother said, "Just a minute, I think I've got him." She slapped her cards down and crowed, then kissed my cheek. Larry gave me a kiss too, on the other cheek. My face was hot.

"Larry's been admiring the Edsel." Now leaning back on the headboard, Mother looked as if she were trying out for a part in a sophisticated comedy.

Larry got up and put his arm around me. "We were thinking we should go for a ride," he said.

"Just give me a minute," Mother said.

Larry and I went into the living room. He said he had been nearby and thought he would surprise me.

"You did." It was the first time he had just showed up like that. I picked up magazines from the floor and piled them on a chair by the table, making a show of rearranging our messiness for the unexpected guest. Then Mother appeared, flushed and expectant, and I softened. I couldn't remember the last time she had been outdoors.

There was an awkward moment at the car. Larry opened the door on the passenger side but Mother was already opening the back door. "Oh no, Mrs. Hupp, you sit up front," he said, in what I considered an overly friendly way. She continued to demur until I snapped, "Just get in, Mother!" Then she said, "You first," but I got in the backseat and slammed the door. There would have been room for all of us in the front, but I didn't like the picture of myself squeezed between my mother and my boyfriend.

I hung over the front seat dangling my arms between them, ashamed of my rudeness. Mother reached over her shoulder and gave my hand a pat. She was enjoying herself. She found a station playing Doris Day and all three of us sang a chorus—*Que sera, sera*—and then groaned. She switched it off.

At a stop sign the car died. Larry said, "Oops." When it happened again, my mother said, "You have to keep one foot on the accelerator pedal while you brake. Just a little."

"That's no good," Larry said, though he kept us moving along by doing exactly as she said. "You need to get the accelerator adjusted."

We drove toward Midland as far as the airport and then turned around and drove home. When we got out, Larry slapped the car like the flank of a horse and said, "Fix that timing, and she'll be a honey."

Mother offered him a soda pop, but it was youth night at his church, where his father was minister, and he had to be there. I walked him to his car. He draped his arms over my shoulders. "How come you don't drive?"

"I'm only fifteen."

"I'll be. Well, you can get a license if you take a course."

"I don't have time to take a course and I wouldn't have a way to get to one anyhow."

"Shoot, get your learner's permit, and I'll teach you, if that's okay with your mother. It'll be easy in her car. You can learn stick shift later on."

"Would you really?"

"We'll go out on lonely roads where you have lots of wiggle room." He bent to touch my forehead with his. His breath, smelling of spearmint, was warm on my face. "And you can thank me by being sweet instead of touchy."

I pulled away. "She's serious sick, you know." Already, her little run of good days was winding down; she was spending most of her time in bed.

"I'm sorry," he said simply. "I was trying to cheer her up. We talked about you." He probably thought I would like that, but I didn't, and my face showed it. "Hey." He lifted my chin with his fingers. "You mad about something?"

"Was she in bed when you came?"

We stood there in stiff silence until he said, "I better go. See you Friday, okay?"

"Okay."

"Would you mind going to a drive-in Saturday? Natalie Wood."

"Why would I?" I said, but I was blushing.

He brushed my hair back from my forehead. "I like your bangs. And I like your mom. I see where you got your smarts. And your good looks."

"Larry?" My voice cracked. "It's nice that you came by. I'm glad she had a little fun." I bounced my head against his chest; I was afraid I would cry if I spoke.

He said, "Do you have any idea how proud of you she is? Music. Debate. Grades. Art. She says you even write poems. She brags and brags."

I pulled back so that I could look at him. "Really?"

"Really." He wrapped me in his arms. "And I was impressed too, kid you not."

When next I called my grandmother, I told her I was dating now, that the boy was a preacher's son, sweet and polite and handsome. I said, "You'd like him," although I knew that was unlikely. She said that I should be careful, that things were not always what they seemed. I knew she meant men. Sight unseen, she meant Larry. Now she would have one more thing to worry about: my heart.

THE NEXT DAY my mother took me downtown to pick up a driver's booklet. A few days later Larry came by and drove the Edsel to the license bureau and waited while I took the written test for a learner's permit. From there we went straight out to a place where there was nothing to see but a few gas pumps and a lot of mesquite. I had my first lesson on a straight dirt road that stank of fresh oil sprinkled to keep the dust down. Driving was easy, once I got the hang of left turns and judging my stops. Larry spoke to me quietly, patiently. I never went more than twenty miles an hour; there was really nothing that could go wrong. The worst possibility would be a jostling ride off the road onto bare dirt. We saw only one other vehicle, a battered pickup; the driver gave us a two-fingered greeting, his hand never lifting from the steering wheel. Larry and I both burst into laughter, mine nearly hysterical with relief from tension I had not known I felt. He said I could drive back to town, but I had had enough.

We got out to switch seats. I waited for him beside the car on the driver's side. I threw my arms around him and gave him a kiss. I pressed hard against his mouth, the effect a sustained smack. Our kisses thus far had all been straightforward, lips to lips, our mouths nearly closed, saliva unmingled. Lately I had felt him loosen, but he had never been soggy or intrusive or demanding, and I had never opened my mouth to him. Sometimes he nibbled my lower lip; I interpreted it as a playful gesture, needing no response other than a giggle or shy retreat. I enjoyed "making out" with him, innocent as it was; the pleasure came from his attention, rather than from any special feelings in my body. I was content to sit close to him, his arm around my shoulders, while we watched a game or a movie, or sat in front of the house at the end of a date. A few times, he had slipped his hands under my shirt, beneath my breasts, never breaching the barrier of my bra. His patience had made me relax my guardedness. I had stopped anticipating the mysterious threshold I was afraid we would cross. Now he leaned back against the car door and drew me close. My abdomen pushed against him and I was aware of the warm bulk inside his jeans. I felt a curious curling in my belly and a feverish giddiness. Gently, he cupped my face with his hands and bent to kiss me. The tip of his tongue darted in my mouth lightly and I tried to respond in the same way. His breath was sweet. My arms dangled because I didn't know where to put them. I was afraid I would touch him in some new, awkward way that made me look foolish, or that I would "give him the wrong idea." My mind whirled. I was so self-conscious, so observing, that my feelings subsided into nothing more than a kind of pride. If this was French-kissing, I did not believe for a minute that it could be a mortal sin. What, exactly, was I getting out of it that was so bad? I wouldn't even say that I liked it, although I liked that I wasn't just a kid to him. For the first time, I could see that a kiss might *lead somewhere*. The Church warned us against the slightest intimacy because we could not be trusted to control ourselves. That was nonsense, I told myself. Maybe some boys could not restrain themselves, but Larry was a minister's son. He respected me. Besides, I was the one who set our limits, just as Rita had advised. And I was so busy monitoring, I certainly wasn't going to lose control.

He wound my hair in his fingers. The gentle tug made my scalp prickle. I thought I would save this moment like a locket to show my mother at the right time.

A FEW DAYS LATER I came home early with a headache. Mother's door was closed. I opened it gently in case she was asleep. She was standing by the window naked. She saw me and waved me away without any particular urgency. Someone was crouched on her bed. I shut the door hurriedly and stood there listening for a few minutes. I was scared something was going on and that she couldn't tell me, but when I heard voices—hers and a man's—they were perfectly calm. I went to my room, too sick with my headache to care any more.

·EIGHT·

I was trying to be an OHS girl. I studied the rich girls who had big photographs in the yearbook: Most Beautiful. Most Friendly. Junior Favorite. I practiced a toothy smile in front of the mirror. I made myself greet my peers; I walked down the middle of the halls now: *Hi. Howzitgoin'?* I was so self-conscious I hardly noticed whether anyone responded. The important thing was to keep going. If Larry could like me, I told myself, someone else could, too.

It started as soon as I got up in the morning. I played the radio in the bathroom while I fixed my hair and put on makeup. Though no one would have guessed it, I modeled my look after the style of a beautiful girl in school, Bitsy Lovelady. I had my bangs trimmed at the beauty parlor and invested in huge rollers I wore to bed at night. I pinned the long hair back into a cascade by contriving two ponytails, one above the other. I used mascara, lipstick, and powder on my nose. Though I hated my child's body, I thought I disguised it with a padded bra and coordinated outfits. Standing in front of the mirror in my underwear, I propped one foot against the side of the other knee, like a stork, and hummed along with the songs on the radio. I left the ironing board up so that I could give a collar or a hem one last hot lick before I dressed. I had become an optimist; in a sea of faces, there had to be a few I could get to know. I longed to crack the code of the girls who stood in huddles until first bell rang, the air around them thick with gossip. How this would happen I had no idea, but the terror of hordes was becoming a tease of possibility: Things could happen here that would never have occurred to me in Catholic school. Now that I was seeing teen movies, I aspired to live their myth: clusters of loyalty, conspiracies of youth against adult stodginess. Adventures. Secrets. Love.

It never, ever happened, but I didn't know it would not. My dream was to be sucked to the center; I had no desire to stand out or stand aside. Oddly, I never stopped to wonder why I met no one through Larry. Did he have no friends of his own, or did he compartmentalize them away from me? We never double-dated; he never introduced me to anyone at the teen center. Now I think maybe he was a loner, biding his time until he could get away, as I would in my next, senior, year.

I did homework in frantic bursts during my solitary lunch hour or surreptitiously in classes where nothing much was going on, so I didn't have to lug books home. Many days I stayed an extra hour to work with the debaters. I had worked on the topic the previous summer and the first three months of the school year, before I left OLV, so I was familiar with the arguments and the general thrust of evidence. I took the case briefs and made them flow more logically. Debaters argued a point and then I showed them how to make it stronger. All this evolved naturally out of a few suggestions, and integrated me into the group. Mrs. Everson hammered into us that we were a team, a family, competing with other schools and not with one another. There was a nice boy who also played tennis, and once in a while James, the object of my admiration, dropped by. It was a nice bunch of kids, but I couldn't think of how to extend my friendship with them to something social, outside school. I don't remember that I even wanted to.

Mrs. Gorman, the English teacher, subscribed to a book club and got three or four new books a month. She brought them in for me. At first it was for extra credit, a little oral report for the class, so that everyone would have a sense of who the contemporary authors were, but credit didn't really have anything to do with it. I read each book in a couple of nights and read the best parts aloud to Mother. I came home from a date with Larry on Friday or Saturday and read until dawn. I gulped authors. Leon Uris, Truman Capote, Pasternak and Camus, Mary McCarthy. I loved Mary Renault and I learned to read Eudora Welty.

As soon as I got home from school, I looked in on Mother. Sometimes she wanted a poached egg or maybe milk toast, something bland and simple. I sat with her while she ate a few bites, then waved the food away. I tried to talk to her, too, but her attention wavered. She lost interest in reading, or lost the energy for it; day after day a book lay open on her bed, pages down. My main concern was that she must be so bored. (Already I didn't see how people could get by if they didn't read.) One day I came home with the exciting news that a triumphant Fidel Castro had entered Havana. It was February 3, 1959, a day of historical importance! Revolution! She said, "That's nice."

I thought maybe reviving her old habits of prayer and spiritual reading might give her heart, a way to find comfort in God, but when I suggested praying or reading, she said, "Let's do it later, honey." She was hardly ever awake more than a couple of hours at a time, though she liked to spend a few minutes with Larry and me before we went out. Sometimes, for that little while, she seemed merely fragile rather than ill, a heroine of another era.

I hoped that if I did my part, God might do his. I had not felt reverent in a while, but I did go to Sunday Mass. I knew that faith could sometimes waver, that you pleased God by remaining steadfast despite your feelings. Even the Little Flower had had her off days. I simply requested a little flexibility. Surely God did not mind that Mother never entered his house; she never left her own.

At Mass I sent up my most earnest supplication: *Show me what to do.* I was coaxing her to eat. I tried to read to her. I offered to fix her hair. *What else? What else?* I prayed. I didn't specifically address Jesus or Mary or one saint or another. I only hoped that someone was listening.

I went to Communion, too, but my old, pious self was being replaced by a pragmatic one. I could feel my mother slipping away, body and soul, and it seemed to me she and I had invested enough in holiness to get back something now. A little practical help, survival.

One day, putting away some laundry in Mother's room, I saw a shoebox I knew was stuffed with photographs and I hauled it out and put it on her bed. Together we looked at a couple dozen pictures of us, mostly of her and me. I wanted to get her to talk about them: *Oh look, remember that was when we stopped at the caves that time,* that sort of thing, but she wasn't much interested. I guessed she was struggling to appear interested at all and I was a little hurt by that, but I stumbled onward, photo after photo.

There I was at First Communion, a beautiful child cast as budding saint. Such big, dark eyes! A lovely dress! And here, another Sunday, with Father Daly beaming beside me. I wore white gloves and a pretty flat hat with a long streamer, a dotted-swiss dress and a dreamy smile. I held it out to her as she picked up a different picture. She sucked in her breath. "What?" I said. Her chin was trembling. She was looking right past me. I reached for it, and she pulled her hand away, but I took it from her.

There was the Mexican child, Davy, in long pants and a crisp white shirt, wearing a sombrero and holding a stuffed bear. You could see that he had been facing away from the camera and someone had called his name. His body was caught in the turn, giving him a startled look. I handed her the photograph quickly.

"My poor little boys," she said, or I thought she said. *Boys?* I didn't challenge her. She often spoke in fragments or in riddles. She often blurted out a phrase with no context, then refused to elaborate. I couldn't tell if her ramblings had any order, any purpose, or were the product of the drugs she took.

She tucked Davy's photograph under all the others, on the bottom of the box. I couldn't remember that child as well as I remembered my grandmother's long-dead dog Tiny, but here was my mother, fixated on his memory, a memory that had nothing to do with me.

"Mother," I said, and she startled.

"Precious child."

I didn't know the right thing to say or do, but I didn't want silence to fill the space between us. Maybe I closed my eyes a moment, like drawing a shade on my resentment, but I knew this was a moment when I might help her, might be what I wanted to be for her, a comfort.

I asked her to tell me about him. When she didn't reply, I started asking questions: Where did he come from? How did you decide to keep him? Who took him away? Why? All the while, she stared at me, hardly blinking, though her eyes were spilling tears. I didn't want her to shut me out. Instinctively I knew if she kept Davy apart and secret, he would occupy a place so special I would never be able to compete with him.

She had to have made a choice, too. She wasn't very strong, and she was tired at that moment; it would have been easier for her to beg off from my questions, but she didn't. She told me what I wanted to know.

This was when I was in boarding school at AMI in Wichita Falls. She hadn't liked the parish priest and had attended Mass at the Mexican church, where she got to know Father Dominguez, the pastor. She had offered her help and he suggested that she volunteer at the day-care center. Davy was a baby there. The father used to drop him off and then he would be the last child picked up. The father was widowed, he had other children, he worked long hours. After a while Mother told him that she could take the baby home overnight sometimes, if he needed for her to. After a while he asked her if she wanted to keep him all the time. He said he had his hands full. Maybe he saw how well the boy was doing with Mother. Maybe he was just worn out. After a couple of months, they agreed that she should file adoption papers. He signed. There was the waiting period.

Then the dead mother's sister got wind of the adoption, and she came up from Mexico and took him. There wasn't anything to be done, because the adoption was not yet final. Mother called the priest and the police and a lawyer, but there was nothing to do except collect his clothes and toys and hug him goodbye. And then, as if there were no end to cruelty, Father Dominguez had been reassigned to another town and replaced by a priest who spoke almost no English. She had lost her baby and her confessor almost in a single stroke.

"Oh Mother," I said, in tears. "I wish I had been here." I crawled up beside her and put my head on her shoulder. She stroked my hair. After a while, both of us dozed.

I SET HER ALTAR up again.

It had been in the front room, by the kitchen, where Karen slept. There was a lamp and some magazines on it. I wiped it clean and moved it to the corner of that same little room. I put a chair by the bed for the lamp, and pulled the spread up on the bed neatly. Karen was getting ready for bed, and I told her she could sleep in my room.

In Mother's closet there was a box with our statue of the Virgin. I found a small, framed photograph of Mother and Karen and me with Father Daly, and a framed holy card of the Little Flower. I arranged everything on the altar. I turned off the light in that room and in the next room, which was the kitchen. The light from the breakfast nook lighted the room dimly. I thought it made it like a chapel, it was such a spare little room.

I took Mother in to see what I had done. She put her hand to the side of her face in a way that thrilled me. "Just a minute," she said. She went back to her room. I waited for several minutes and then became uneasy, but I met her in the living room as she made her way back. She was carrying a large candle in a glass holder decorated with a picture of the Virgin of Guadalupe, a snake crushed beneath her feet. On the back was the "Oracion a la Milagrosa," a prayer to Mary. I made a space for the candle on the altar.

Mother sat down on the bed, her hands on each side of her gripping the mattress as if she had not made up her mind to stay or go. I asked her if she wanted to say the Rosary. She didn't answer right away. That made me nervous and I said, "If you don't want to, that's okay." She held up her hand to shush me. She moved over on the bed, closer to the window, and spread apart two slats of the blinds to look outside. She turned from the window and motioned for me to sit beside her. It reminded me of that day so long ago when we had sat just like this, our backs to the headboard, our legs out straight, and we had talked about kisses. I wondered if she remembered, too. Now she said, "I'm awfully tired tonight. Let's say one Hail Mary, slowly. Tomorrow I'll look for my *Imitation of Christ,* and you can read to me from it in the evening. Would you like that?"

I said I would and we said the Hail Mary and then we just sat there in the quiet dark. I hoped she would forget Davy so that she wouldn't grieve for him, and I hoped that we would have a few more moments before Tommy came, but I heard him turn the corner onto our street almost right away. There was the flicker from his headlights shining through the window blinds as he came up the driveway. My mother's excitement was almost palpable. She gave me a little push and I got off the bed and she did too. She kissed my forehead and she said, "You are going to be a big girl for me, aren't you? I can count on you?" and I said I would try. I had hated that phrase, *big girl,* because I had always thought it was a way of saying I was a child, but suddenly I realized that what she meant was *I need for you not to need me anymore.* It was a lot to promise, but for that little while, I thought I could do it.

ONE DAY I CAME HOME and found her sleeping in a bed streaked with her blood. Karen was with her, her face purple from crying. She said Tommy was on his way.

Tommy and I helped her walk to the bathroom, where we cleaned her. The wounds on her wrists were superficial, despite the blood. Tommy wrapped gauze and tape around the wounds and we set her in her wing-back chair across from the foot of the bed. Karen stood by her side in case she slumped. Tommy helped me change the bed. I piled the bloody sheets on the floor, and he told me to take them out to the garbage barrels by the alley. A few days later, he brought new sheets and gave them to me in another room, away from Mother's attention. He said I shouldn't worry. "It's my job."

"So you've said." I wanted to blame him for her decline, but in my heart I knew that he was doing all he could.

That night, I heard her moaning. I crawled up onto the bed beside her and stroked her arm and her hip, whispering, *Mary, Mother of God, watch over us,* until she slept.

After that, I was more watchful. While she waited for Tommy, I lay on her bed, reading. When he came, I stayed awake in my room, listening for his departure, and then I lay beside her until I was sure she was fast asleep. I learned to breathe her sour smell without minding.

·

I WAS FINALLY DESPERATE enough to go see Father Lyndale, the pastor Mother didn't like. I told him that she was very ill, and that she had lost her spirit. I felt almost disloyal, but I wanted him to bring Communion to her. He said he would as soon as she called to say she wanted him to come.

"I don't know if she will do that," I said. "I mean, I don't know if she can."

"Is she unconscious?"

"Not unconscious, no, but not reasonable, either."

"Is she dying?"

I was shocked. "No, it's a lapse, a spell, it's a bad time she's going through."

He looked at his watch. He went to a file cabinet and took out some papers. He gave them to me—brochures with prayers, poor reproductions of images of Mary. He wanted me to take them to her and to tell her to call him anytime. Or if she was worse, he said, I could call.

In the parking lot, I tore the pamphlets into tiny pieces and scattered them in the gritty wind.

· · ·

It was early March. Larry and I went to see Sandra Dee and Troy Donahue in *A Summer Place*. I didn't even know who they were. Larry told me about the movie *Gidget,* then assured me that he had heard that the movie was romantic, serious, "just up your alley." He had said that about Natalie Wood and Gene Kelly in *Marjorie Morningstar*, and he had been right. I didn't really care. We turned bad films into opportunities to mock. Mocking was our favorite pastime.

He headed for the middle section, where families parked and the light from the concession stand would fall on us. I craned my neck to see the line of cars along the back fence, where all the couples sank low in their seats, where they disappeared after intermission. My peers. I didn't think of them that way. They knew things I did not.

I put my hand on Larry's arm. "We could park a little farther back. There's always somebody blocking the picture." He gave me a sly, sideways look. He moved three rows back, away from the concession stand. He fiddled with the microphone; pop music played until the feature started. He couldn't lower the volume enough to suit him. I said, "You're sitting right against the speaker. Come over here. The sound will be just right." He slid away from the steering wheel to the center of the seat.

I tugged at his elbow. He scooted closer and I climbed over him. I was wearing a hand-me-down cashmere sweater Aunt Mae had given me, and a gray light-wool skirt, straight to my knees, with a kick pleat, and I had to pull it up some to get across him. As I slid over, he put his hands on my knees to steady me, and then on my thighs, higher, and just for an instant, I froze, like someone in a photograph; for the first time, I felt that sweet shock between my legs. For just a moment, I had only the one thought: *More.* Then I rearranged my skirt and pressed my knees together. Gently, as if I were a child going to bed, he pulled off my loafers, and I moved my legs up onto the seat, tucking them sideways carefully, fussing with my skirt. The places where he had touched me still held the delicate surprise of skin on skin, the ghost of the pressure of his thumbs. I stared straight ahead, waiting for the movie to start. He slipped his arm around me and I fell limply against him. The cartoon splashed onto the screen and he bent down and thrust his tongue between my teeth.

A SUMMER PLACE is a melodramatic romance, greatly helped along by its theme song, which was enormously popular for at least a year. It opens when Troy Donahue's family (he is Johnny) approaches a Maine island on their yacht, and he spies Sandra Dee (Molly) on shore. By nightfall they are kissing in the boat shed. They get caught in a storm on an island and are out all night. Hell breaks loose; Molly's mother hauls her to a doctor. The young lovers are immediately separated and sent to boarding schools, where of course they have telephones.

Together again clandestinely, their urgency escalates. "Is kissing me enough?" she asks him. There's some back and forth about being good. "Have you been bad, Johnny? Have you been bad with other girls?" she asks him. Her face scrunches up with the anguish of her inner conflict. Should she, should she not—hardly a real question.

It would have been embarrassing, except that Larry didn't like it, either. We made little comments all the way through, mostly about how obvious all the hints were. He remarked that Troy Donahue had a fat chin and the bewildered gaze of an old dog, and I said that Sandra Dee was impossibly sweet. Every emotion was carried by the swelling theme song. The story was obvious. Sandra and Troy are united. In retrospect, I suppose it was an unusual movie, because everyone who loved someone won out, even though they broke all the rules. For 1959, that was daring.

Larry's clowning had a physical aspect. Johnny would embrace Molly, and Larry would move his hand up and down my back. They would kiss, and he would kiss the back of my neck with smooching sound effects. I giggled and tried to have a good time, but by the end of the movie I was tense and tired. The exaggerated mimicry had an edge of frenzy that sucked my energy and alarmed me. I thought this must be what it was like to get drunk. I knew I would lose my equilibrium if I did not stay sober, and I did not want to think where the falling would stop.

WE DROVE OUT OF TOWN, into the same area where he had taught me to drive Mother's Edsel, out where there was nothing to see but a few gas pumps and a lot of mesquite.

It was a cold, clear night, and the landscape had the eerie luminescence of a dream. Larry pulled off the road and parked the car, pointed toward a pump-jack that wasn't operating. It looked like a giant, prehistoric insect. Far off, a windmill rose beside an open water tank, the sort of place boys went on summer nights to douse themselves with their naked buddies, no girls allowed.

He didn't touch me. He just looked. I couldn't read his face, and I had no idea what he saw in mine. We sat like that for a minute or two—it seemed forever—and then he said, "Are you a good girl?"

My face prickled with shock. What was the right answer? I said lightly, "Good as I know how," and instantly I knew it was a stupid thing to say, rife with innuendo I did not intend or even fully understand. To my relief, he laughed softly, leaned back, and beckoned with his finger. *Come here.*

I curled against him, snug under his arm. My chest was tight. I concentrated on my breathing. He took his glasses off and set them on the dashboard, and waited. When I repositioned myself so that we could kiss, he whispered, "You know you don't have to be afraid of me, don't you? You know I'm a good guy?" I could smell his aftershave. Without his glasses, he looked dreamy and distracted. Instead of replying, I took the initiative to kiss him. He did nothing, as if he were asleep, and I took this as a dare. I kissed him calculatedly, until he had to respond: a little teasing, a luxurious, long kiss, a nip; a still moment, and then my tongue, bold against his, and that shock of surprise at myself again, as I discovered that I knew just how to do it, and that it was lovely to reach him in this liquid way. I thought that I was losing the boundary of my lips, I was folding into him. Happiness surged in me like carbonation. It wasn't sex, it was power: I sensed his surprise and nervous delight.

He ran his hands down my sides, onto the slight curve of my hips. My hands were planted on his shoulders, palms against his chest. He said my name. I could push or pull. Say yes or no. But not knowing where the edge was—that was the thrill. His hands slid over me. It was a wonderful sensation. He pulled the sweater up from my waist and moved his hands beneath my breasts. One of his thumbs pressed upward. I stiffened. I was wearing a padded bra, and he had pushed into the cushioning foam. I twisted up and to the side, so that his hand slid off of the brassiere. He reached around to the back and unclasped the hooks. The brassiere sprang away from my flat chest, probably a lot less obviously than I felt it did, but I was mortified. I was fifteen, with the body of a tall ten-year-old. I pulled back, in effect giving him better access. He pressed both hands against me. I wrenched away.

"Hey," he said.

I wanted to scream, *Don't you ever say anything but "hey"?* I struggled to hook the bra, and when I couldn't, I began to cry. He did it for me. He rubbed my back. "Hey," he said again.

I turned around and glared at him. Through my tears, he looked frightening and unfamiliar. He stuck his head forward and tried to kiss me as he moved his hands under my bunched-up skirt onto my thighs. I shoved him away. Then I crushed myself against my door, trying to make myself small. I thought of my nipples against his palms and they tingled.

"You think I care if you don't have big headlights?" He was leaning against his door now. We were like broken bookends.

"I want to go home." I would never forgive his choice of words.

He put his glasses on again and sighed. "This is crazy," he said. "I didn't mean that. You're pretty as can be. I'm just rattled. I'm sorry. Jeez. You think any of this stuff matters?"

He reached for me, and when I resisted, he scooted closer. There was room on the front seat for a girl to lie beneath a boy. I pressed my back hard against the door, my body twisted, my feet not quite on the floor. He tried to put his arm around me, and when he couldn't do that, he put both hands on the windowglass behind my head, and leaned in and kissed me. There wasn't any place to escape. The easiest thing was to yield, and I did, relieved to stop resisting. He pulled my legs up onto the seat and lay on top of me. I knew nothing about what we were doing, but I realized that there was nothing I had to know. I was weary and resigned, as if I had gone to sleep and wakened years later. I trembled and he clasped me tightly. He made no effort to undo my clothing, or his own, he simply held me fast. He trembled slightly. I was breathing shallowly in small gasps like those a child makes before bursting into tears. I felt his sex against me, his breath on my neck, but I knew he was a better boy than Johnny. He wouldn't do this unless I said it was okay. Maybe not then. I didn't know what fears his father, Reverend Predmore, had instilled in him.

Everything my friend Rita had ever said raced through my mind. How boys went so far and then couldn't stop. How it was up to the girls to put the brakes on before they got crazy, before they got *blue balls*. She hadn't said anything about what this would be like for me; how I would want to see what it felt like to touch a man's sex. How I wanted him to touch me, too.

There would never be a moment in my life so big or so terrible (and there have been terrible moments) that I would not be able to imagine it even as it happened. There would never be a significant dialog without quotation marks in my head. I lead two lives, one ordinary and clumsy, the other an overlay of observation. When my feelings are flattened by my fear of them, I can always say what's happening, as if I am committing my life to memory for a test. At every turn, I see alternative possibilities, multiple interpretations, and although I have sometimes resented the ambiguity, I have also relished my otherness. Every picture is a scrim over another. It took me many years to discover the humor and wickedness in my peculiar sightedness, let alone to dare to think of it as a talent, but even early on, I cast it on everything and turned my life side to side as I lived it. Is that good or bad? Does it matter?

I didn't understand any of this at fifteen, of course. I didn't understand it that night when I was caught up in a frenzy of conflicting emotions, riding them on a chute of physical sensation.

Larry, he a Baptist minister's son, was waiting for me, the

Catholic girl, to stop us, *to stop what we were doing;* that was my part in our sexual exploration. I didn't want the responsibility. What decisions had I ever made? Uniformed since the age of seven, I hadn't even chosen my own school clothes until two months ago.

"Larry, Larry," I whimpered, holding my arms out. *Make it okay.* I must have looked like a child wanting to be picked up. I thought my vulnerability would disarm him, but I wore it clumsily.

He wouldn't look at me. *"Smart girls."* His disgust thudded like a heavy door slammed shut. There was no place for all my feelings to go, and so they turned outward again, barbed and resentful.

"That movie," I said, "was *stupid.* I *hate* Sandra Dee." I made my voice high, insipid, like hers, *"Johnny, have you been a bad boy? Have you been bad with girls?* When that was *exactly* what she wanted him to be!"

We needed to just go home and pretend this hadn't happened. I felt that he had tricked me, with all his joking around during the movie, his complicity in my scorn. He had tricked me into revealing myself before I knew who I was. Of course that's how most of us stumble through adolescence, but nobody thinks that at the time. Everything matters so much. Then, as now, teenagers died of humiliation, thwarted desire, lack of vision.

In and out, the sound of his breath, the sound of mine. He said, "That's what you hated, wasn't it? She did what she wanted to do. She wasn't scared to death of sex. She's the same age as you, and she has that body. *And you wish you were just like her."*

Even now I can remember my indignation. His words play in my mind like a tape. Never mind that he was insulting my body. That he wanted to hurt my feelings. I did truly hate Sandra Dee. I hated that she was someone boys wanted. I hated the part she had been given to play—her character's wealth, and the absolute certainty of her attraction to that big lunky boy, the humiliation of her mother's assault on her dignity, the cliché of her pregnancy and the stupid happy ending. I felt sorry for her. If Larry thought I was jealous of her, he had me all wrong. People were always misunderstanding me; how could I be close to him if he was no better?

"I want to go home," I said again. It took forever. I had to scrabble for my shoes. My sweater was twisted, my hair was a mess. I kept glancing at Larry, but I never caught him looking at me. At the curb in front of my house, I opened the door, but he grabbed my arm.

"Wait, please, I'm sorry."

I wrenched my arm away and got out of the car. He jumped out and followed me to the door. He slammed his hand against the screen so that I couldn't pull it open. I faced the door, so that he had to talk to the back of my head. He leaned in and his breath stirred my hair.

"I don't do that. I won't. Heck, I'm a virgin, too." *Pause.* "I'll deny it if you tell."

I whirled around. "You think this is a joke? I never want to see you again. How could you think I was jealous of Sandra Dee?"

He stepped back and I pushed my way inside and slammed the door.

The house was completely dark. I stood still and waited for my eyes to adjust. I thought of the way I had kissed him, and I shuddered with revulsion. *He made me do it,* I told myself, but I knew full well he had not.

The hall light went on. Mother came around the corner. "Sweetie, it's you?" It was cold in the house, but she was wearing a summery gown that rustled about her knees as she hurried toward me.

I tried to speak, but instead of words, a squeak came out of me, the first syllable of my fury.

"Oh darling," she said, a little clumsy with her arms out. "Whatever happened? Whatever's made you so upset? Come to me. Come to your mother."

Karen appeared, lagging behind her, hovering in the doorway, giving me that appraising look.

Mother wrapped her arms around me and pressed her face into my hair. "Come sleep with me," she said.

The luxury of her embrace flooded me with relief. A warmth spread out from my chest into my limbs. My anger washed away but I was left with my stiff resolve. Tomorrow, I thought, I would tell her how he had insulted me, I would tell her I hated him and would never see him again. I would not tell her how wrong he had been about me, how much I had wanted him to show me what could happen next. I knew she would have understood completely what I meant, but I knew too that she did not think I was ready to have such wants. She wanted me to be grown-up when I needed to be, but still to be her little girl. I wanted to tell her that nobody can be two things at once. I wanted to ask her to help me choose one, for now, whichever would make her most want to be my mother.

That night when I came home full of indignation about Sandra Dee was the last time I held my mother close. I was a teenager, worst luck, with thin skin and a thick skull. I had a chip on my shoulder that rolled off and landed between my mother and me. There wasn't time left to go around.

. . .

Two weeks went by and I heard nothing from Larry. Mother asked me why I didn't call him. *Because I don't have his number!* I said. *Because I don't want to!*

My grandmother planned a weekend trip from Wichita Falls. That meant that I could go to a speech tournament in Austin. We were leaving at noon on Friday. Aunt Mae said she would come over to spend the night with Mother and Karen, since my grandmother wouldn't arrive until mid-morning on Saturday. Everyone was enthusiastic about my going. I couldn't get to sleep, I was so excited at the prospect of the competition, and the trip, too: five girls were going to share one motel room.

I took the car home at lunch time; the speech teacher, Mrs. Everson, would pick me up soon after. I hoped Mother was awake to hug me and wish me luck. My head was stuffed with news and the opinions of columnists; I was excited about extemporaneous speaking, the event that attracted the most aggressive contestants.

Larry's car was parked in front of the house. I ran up the walk and burst into the living room. He and Mother were sitting at the table with empty bowls in front of them. She was wearing her chenille robe and she hadn't penciled on her eyebrows. It was the first time I had seen her up in days and days.

She said, "There's tomato soup on the stove."

"You cooked?" It was a sarcastic question and she didn't bother to answer. But heating a can of soup was more than she had done in a month.

I turned my attention to Larry. "Don't you go to school anymore?" I glared at him. I felt a headache strike me in my left eye. It hurt so much I brought my hand up to cover it.

Mother said, "I bet you're hungry."

"It's lunch time," Larry said.

"At my house? You came to lunch at my house?" I made myself take my hand off of my eye. I could feel my eyelid dancing.

Larry shrugged. Mother said, "He brought me some magazines, isn't that sweet?"

"I wondered how you all are," he said. I had been waiting for him to come to his senses, and he hadn't called. I didn't even realize I had been waiting until I saw him sitting there with my mother.

"I have to pack." I fled to my room and slammed the door. My bag was ready, sitting by the door. I threw myself on my bed, the throbbing side of my head down in the pillow. I heard Larry leave, and in a few minutes Mother came and sat down on the bed.

"You've got a migraine," she said. She brushed my hair off my face. "Are you up to this?"

I sat up. "What was he doing here? I thought you were so *sick*."

She looked at me for a long moment. I don't know how she kept from slapping me or just walking away, except that she lacked the energy, and she loved me, and she was a grown-up. Larry's visit had tired her, and now I was using up strength she didn't have to spare.

"Honey, I think he misses you. He's a nice boy. Really, he is."

"He didn't know I would be here. He came to see you."

She sighed. "He just wanted to talk. He wanted to know if you would see him again. He didn't believe an argument about a movie could be so serious."

"I guess he knows now."

I wanted so much to go back to the beginning with Larry and make it turn out another way. I missed him and I hated him for it. I couldn't see that I was doing the same thing now with Mother, the old mountain out of a molehill I'd heard about all my childhood. Overreacting. Tripping on my lower lip.

Hurting my mother and unable to stop.

You always think you can straighten it out later on.

She said, "I know he would like to apologize." So she had been sorry to see him go, too. Did she see what I could not, that I wasn't going to have more Larrys come along? Not ever?

"He said that? He wants to apologize?"

"In so many words."

I fell back on my pillow again. "You go out with him, Mother. I don't want to."

She winced, then exhaled wearily, but she would not be provoked.

She went away for a few minutes. I heard her opening a drawer in her bedroom and closing it again. She went into the kitchen, too.

She laid a big envelope on the end of my bed. "These are for you," she said. "To look at when you feel better." I pushed the envelope with my foot.

She sat beside me once more. "Here's an ice pack, darling. Put it on your eye, it'll help." She bent to kiss me. On my lips, I think.

Getting up, she moaned.

I put the envelope in my drawer without looking. It held her photographs, of course. My grandmother found them when we were packing and took them to her house. I finally looked at them one of the summers between college years, and what came back wasn't my walking in on her nakedness. It was the day she gave them to me. I'll always wonder why she chose that day. I was angry. I was leaving for the weekend.

What did she have in mind to do?

ALL THE WAY to Austin, I slept, and though the headache had drained me, I was able to do the round of competition that evening, and by the time we were at the motel, I was fine. I enjoyed all the turn-taking and the talking in the dark. I shared a bed with Lynelle Wood. She had a sweet disposition, a fantastically high hairline, and huge breasts. I'd heard jokes that went like this: *Lynelle Wood, Lynelle Wood, Lynelle would let you touch them.* Lying beside her, I wondered if she had heard them, too. We had talked about being partners for our senior year. She was smart and intense, like me.

Saturday, I won first place, beating girls from Houston and Dallas schools, girls with extravagant gestures, who wore expensive suits and regarded us West Texas girls with disdain. One of our boys placed in persuasive oratory, and Lynelle and her partner reached the quarterfinals. I heard that debate, and I thought that Lynelle and I would have won. Next year, we would. I was actually looking forward to something at school.

The night was balmy. At the motel, there were other kids wandering around, some of them from the speech meet, and boys in town for a wrestling tournament. The motel was built on a hilly plot. It was fun, walking up and down; I lived in a place where the land extended flat and open to the horizon. I found a pop machine and ended up talking for a long time to a cute boy from Snyder. We took our drinks around the corner behind bushes, leaning against the side of one of the units. I took little sips from my bottle until they were warm and flat. Every time I lifted the bottle to my lips, I thought of the pose I made. I cocked my hip, as if my drink knocked me off balance. He rolled his tee shirt up like James Dean and gave me puffs of his cigarette. We inched our way closer and closer to one another, until our hips bumped, and he laid his arm across my shoulders. We were in a place private enough for a game of sorts, but there wasn't any place where we could go too far. Perfect boundaries. We didn't know anything about one another; he didn't care if I was smart or popular or virgin, he just liked the smell of my hair (he said so) and I liked the smooth skin over the ripple of his wrestler's muscles. I started running my hand up and down his arm. A warm languor spread through me, as if I would melt, or float away. I stole glances at his crotch; he moved so that I couldn't see the way he strained against his tight jeans. He pretended to be interested in my speech event, though I could tell he had no idea what I was talking about. We exchanged names and telephone numbers on scraps of paper, but I knew that I would never see him again. He kissed me good bye. We pushed our bodies against one another but held our hands lightly on shoulders, like polite dancers. When I got back to the room, and Lynelle said they had started to worry, all I could do was grin.

While I waited for my turn in the bathroom, I called home collect to tell my mother that I had won. Aunt Mae answered.

"Guess what? I won."

"That's so good," she said. She sounded weary.

"Did Mommy get there okay? Will she have to leave before I get home? Tell her not to."

Aunt Mae said, "Don't worry about Mommy, she's going to stay."

My face stung as if I had been slapped. I knew very well what it meant: that my grandmother was back in Odessa to stay. "Is Mother awake? I want to tell her—"

"No, baby, she was so tired tonight. You can tell her about it tomorrow, okay?"

"But I want her to know that I'm sorry," I said. "It's important. Please!" I was spinning into panic. I wanted to shout: *This isn't a good time for this!* "Can't you tell her that for me? *I'm sorry?* Tell her tonight? Tell her *now?*"

"You sleep tight," Aunt Mae said. "I've got to go." I cried out, "No, wait!" but she hung up. I looked up and saw that my roommates were all looking at me.

"Your turn," Lynelle said softly, pointing toward the bathroom. I took a bath, lying back with my eyes shut until the water cooled. When I was done, the girls were all in bed and the lights were out. I got into bed and pulled my knees up to my chest. I dug at my feet furiously, scratching away flecks and bits of flesh, tearing long strips of skin from the pads of my heels, until Lynelle, sweet and patient as she was, had had enough and huffed to let me know so. I closed my hands into fists and tucked them against my cheeks, and I tried to pray.

. . .

Mother told me once that she counted herself among the blessed, that that was the gift of faith, and that it helped her get through bad days. She liked to say that the great saints had seduced her, not so much because they convinced her of anything as that she thought that if they could believe, so could she.

I believe that, right up to the end, she was trying—trying to believe and hope, trying to find meaning in her pain, trying not to be afraid, trying to broker heavenly attention to her children. She survived, day to day, defying that worst calamity, the terrible surety of her total absence, until it could no longer be resisted. Why else would she use a good day to record her presence in nude photographs, except to cling to life, to celebrate it?

I think that when she got in the taxi that December day and went to the hospital, she spoke out of pain, yes, but also frustration and anxiety about the future—her children's future more than hers. I think when she cried out, she meant that she couldn't be what she wanted to be for us, and it wasn't fair. Maybe once she had dreamed of being a movie star or a politician or a doctor's wife, but I believe that for all our lives, she wanted to be our mother.

I COULDN'T HELP seeing the cuts on her arms. She spent hours trimming her cuticles with a razor blade. She didn't cut deeply, it was more a thin, red tracing that beaded, scabbed lightly, and left pale white threads of scars. I wanted to touch them, but I pretended not to notice. Alongside the scars, she made new incisions. I tried not to be alarmed by her cutting after Tommy told me not to be, but I wished she would stop. She was deliberate and absorbed rather than reckless. She had done the cutting for years, and some times she had done it more seriously and decisively, but now she merely dabbed at the threads of welling blood. There was no more blood on the bed. Today we call this "self-cutting," an activity especially favored by young women who prefer the pain they impose on themselves over other pain they perceive as unbearable, but in 1959 we didn't know what to make of it. And I think there is another explanation.

I thought it was idleness that provoked her, that she was seeking a surcease from boredom. It did not occur to me that she might have mutilated herself, not for distraction, but for the possibility of ecstasy.

THE LAST FEW DAYS of her life, she lost her words. Her poems and prayers and worries were all gone in a slur. She stumbled in the hallway and slid down the wall. *Osh, murf, plzt, mu,* she said. She lay in a stupor but a day later tried again: *cul ba prees,* tears leaking down her temples into her hair and behind her ears. She slipped away from words into a coma, but I swore I saw her lips moving at the end. I have spent a lifetime wondering what she said.

On the morning she died, she received Extreme Unction, a sacramental anointing, administered by the pastor she did not like, who was barely able to disguise his disinterest in her death, but by then she was unconscious. She was unable to receive the "last sacrament," a final Eucharist to feed her fleeing soul. At least she was beyond the reach of the priest's condescension, as she was beyond the reach of our cries: *Don't go!* My grandmother, mute with grief, wobbled and grasped the bedpost. She said, *Not here.* She couldn't have meant the dying, and nobody would want to bury Mother in Odessa. Maybe she meant to say, *Not now.*

Don't go!

·

TOMMY SAID he didn't think she should go to the hospital. In the hospital, she couldn't have her children with her.

We were all with her at home except Uncle Howard, who was in the field. My uncle Sonny came with his wife, Twyla, from East Texas. Aunt Mae, of course, thirty years old and reeling from grief and responsibility. Her children. Our cousin Joan remembers Mother in the hall coming out of the bathroom, stumbling and then sliding down the wall into someone's arms. Karen held Joan's hand and stood out of the way until near the end.

Mother died in the early hours of Wednesday, March 25, 1959. Until I looked at the death certificate, while I was working on this manuscript, I thought she died on Good Friday. She was thirty-three and it always seemed so perfect to me, a sign from Jesus that I couldn't figure out. I had a twinge of disappointment when I saw the date, but it passed. What does it matter except that she is gone?

I was sitting in the wing-back chair at the foot of her bed. I had been in that very place for most of two days, snarling at Aunt Mae when she suggested I get some rest in a bed. The priest had come and gone. Mother lay on her back, still except for her labored breathing, her head turned slightly to the right, toward the window. Someone had brushed her hair. Her skin had a gray pallor, but I did not think that she was ugly. I did not think that she was fighting anything and I thought that her restful patience would give her time to gain new strength, to come back to us, recharged. And oh, we would understand now how much she hurt! We would give her everything she asked for: quiet and dark, drugs, our softest voices.

There was a noise from her (no movement), but I can't remember what it was like. I'm confused by all the deathbed narratives I've read: grunts and sighs, honks and whistles, most often a rattle. I just know that we knew, all of us, and do not think that it was a relief. Tommy was beside her and he looked around at us, his face slack and damp. My grandmother, swaying with shock, slumped against Aunt Mae. Nobody was available to anyone else; our stunned grief had a melded sound, low and garbled, a murmuring as if in an exotic tongue, punctuated by yips from my sister, who squatted just inside the closet a few feet from the bed. I grasped the curled knobs on the ends of the chair arms with such force, the palms of my hands were bruised for days. I couldn't make myself get up to go to my mother, although I longed to touch her one more time. I couldn't believe that she was doing this. I thought, *Wake up, Mama, call me and I'll come over there.* I thought, *Open your eyes, Mama, I'm sitting in your chair.* I couldn't make myself leave it and travel to her bed. I thought if I didn't give in, she would snap out of it, like a game I didn't want to play.

The wind began to howl, or maybe for the first time in days I remembered that the world went on outside my mother's room. The bad weather was right and it pleased me. This was March on the plains of West Texas; the sand, swept by fiercely stuttering winds, was so thick there was no sky, no sun. It blew all day, and in the afternoon, some rain fell, so that cars were spattered with mud.

A moment passed and my grandmother's keening called up everyone's crying, each of us wailing in our own minor key. It was awful to hear. I ran outside and drove the Edsel to school, leaning close to the steering wheel, holding on tight. I went through the halls looking for Rita. A teacher saw me and said, *Why aren't you in class?*

My mother died!

I looked in the windows of classrooms. My trig teacher came to the door and I said, *My mother died!* then ran on. I couldn't remember Rita's schedule. The teacher from the hall found me again and led me, gently, to the office. In a few minutes Rita appeared, sobbing. She went to my house with me. My grandmother was sedated. Twyla was scrambling eggs. Someone had come to take Mother away.

EVERYTHING THAT MY GRANDMOTHER was able to carry out of Mother's house went into her own. Her clothes, crammed in the closet in the second bedroom and in garment bags in the hall, smashed against the hot-water heater. Her silverware, accrued one piece at a time over years, black with tarnish, wrapped in velvet bags and tied with ribbons, stored in a wooden chest under the bed. Boxes of books. Scratchy woolen squares on string worn around the neck for penance; rosaries and crucifixes; the ceramic statue of Mary. Colored pencils and tiny tubes of watercolors. Old cracked makeup, dishes. My grandmother built a storage shed in the backyard of her house to hold the overflow. She put the best things in boxes between the bed and the wall in her second bedroom. At the foot of the bed was my mother's cedar chest, filled with papers, photographs, albums, and clippings. For what? I used to think, but when I slept in my grandmother's house, years later, I lay each night and faced the boxes, and I wondered what had happened to her notebooks; I wondered what she had written. Maybe she had said goodbye. Maybe she said she was sorry. If I had her words, I thought, I would know who she had been.

The notebooks were the only things I wanted, but by the time my grandmother and I cleared out Mother's room, they had disappeared. I suppose Daddy burned them. I suppose they frightened him: her secrets and fears, the blame, her longing and disappointment. It was the first time he stood up for himself. The next time was at the funeral, when he wouldn't let us sit with Mother's kin. Then he left, boldest move of all.

NINE

This is what happens when a person dies of renal failure. The kidneys falter; blood fills with impurities; other organs are poisoned, including the brain. Yet death does not usually warn the patient or her loved ones; it does not come on gradually like a clock slowing down. Instead, the patient suddenly slips into coma or suffers heart failure or a stroke. While every day for a long time seemed like a vigil against a distant end, you took no opportunity to say goodbye. What you should have known was coming arrives instead as a shock, as if the ill person were struck by a car on the curb. The events seem untidy and you feel careless. There is so much left unsaid. The whole thing is an insult.

What did you think was going on?

I did some research, trying to understand what my mother was going through during her years of illness. I tried to get her hospital records, but wasn't successful. I learned that an autopsy was required by Texas state law when a person died at home, so I tried to get an autopsy report but I was unable to locate one, even with the date of death and other pertinent information. When I consulted my aunt, she said that an autopsy had not been performed, law or no law—such a long illness, such a respected physician.

I do have a copy of the death certificate. It says that she died of kidney abscesses of long standing. More technically, this condition is *suppurative nephritis,* in which infected tissue liquefies and forms pus. The only treatment is antibiotics, sometimes coupled with draining of abscesses. I am sure that Mother was given antibiotics, along with painkillers and sedatives. All in all, treatment for her condition at that time was primitive.

The term for the chronic condition that I heard as a child, Bright's disease, used to refer to several types of inflammatory kidney disease, and wasn't really accurate in her case; it is no longer in general use. *Glomerulonephritis,* as it is more properly called, is believed to be an allergic reaction to bacterial infections elsewhere in the body, such as strep throat or scarlet fever (she probably had both). The symptoms—chills, fever, vomiting, fatigue, and abdominal and flank pain—all appear in Mother's symptoms and history. You can think of it as the launching and then the cruise control of her lifetime of illness, something that started in childhood and accounted for her frailty as an adolescent, continuing as a chronic condition that led to death. I read that with bed rest, antibiotics, and dietary restrictions, 95 percent of patients recover from the acute phase, that is, the first onset of the disease. The failure of

early treatment, or the persistence of the disease despite treatment, results for the other 5 percent in renal damage and eventually in death.

As I read the descriptions in the medical literature, my first
reaction was to think that if she did die of an overdose—I assumed
she had taken everything she had in the house—she had good reason. I realized, with shame and sorrow, how little awareness I had
had of the severity of her pain. I was always so focused on her state
of alertness, her unsteady gait, and her lethargy, I hardly considered her pain, and she never said anything about it to me, nor did
any adult. And all her talk of my maturity—that I was her *big girl*—
was an indication that she thought that we would be all right without her. I imagined her asking herself, *What good am I to anyone?
How much more can I suffer?* There was no note. She gave no
warning. I based my awful assumption that she committed suicide
on my guilt and grief, and on the suddenness of her death. None
of us were prepared for it; how could it have been a natural death?
I had thought that she would spend many more years up and
down, then fade away like someone whose batteries ran out. I
completely misunderstood the nature of her illness.

I didn't think, "She committed suicide," or "She killed herself."
I thought, "She gave up." That she would do so while I was away
from her and when we had a misunderstanding hovering between
us seemed a betrayal, a deliberate denial of my opportunity to put
things right for my sake. Besides, it flew in the face of my efforts
to keep her connected to me, to life, and to her faith. Suicide
tossed all aside. It was proof that I didn't matter enough to her.

So it was that her death, like most things, seemed to be about
me. Even now, at my age, having raised a child and having taught
hundreds of kids, knowing that self-centeredness is practically a

description of adolescence, it's hard to forgive myself my solipsism, but I remind myself that I was the one I hurt. I don't know if my sister had these impressions at the time, but I'm almost positive she developed them over the years and that she still is convinced that Mother abandoned her. She won't discuss it, won't hear a word about our mother, and I'm sure she won't read my book.

One sad postscript: While I was writing this, I talked it over with my aunt, and she said, "No way did Edith die of an overdose. Heavens, she had just refilled a big bottle of painkillers, and it was still sitting in the medicine cabinet unopened." She (Mae) had wondered what to do with it, and finally had just thrown it away.

For want of an unasked question, two daughters' grief goes awry.

A YEAR OR SO before my grandmother died, she told me that she always thought that Tommy Miller murdered Mother. (And *now* I think of him as Tommy!) Trying to hide my astonishment, speaking gently, I urged her to explain. She said that shortly before Mother died, she had heard her say, "Police," feebly, to be sure, but clearly. I pointed out that I had always been sure that she had said, "Priest," and that I had called Father Lyndale, believing that Mother wished to receive last rites.

My grandmother had further argument for her belief. In the fall of 1959, she had begun training as a licensed vocational nurse at Odessa Junior College. As she learned about symptoms of many kinds, she reflected on Mother's death and arrived at the conclusion that it was the result of a drug overdose. It was something about her pupils. She remembered Tommy giving Mother an injection late in the evening some hours before she lapsed into a coma. She thought the coma had been deliberately induced.

"Why in the world would he do that?" I asked. "He loved her!"

My grandmother said that Mother had become a burden to him, or maybe he saw it as a mercy killing. She believed, as I do now, that if Mother had had earlier, more aggressive care, her condition would not have deteriorated to the state that she would die so young. What we can't know is where the line was crossed, when it was that chronic nephritis became irreversible. I am glad that it didn't occur to my grandmother that the "fault" may have lain, at least in part, in her own ignorance and poverty; in the inconsistency of Mother's treatment and the disinterest of doctors; in the failure of a system to care for a poor woman—all culpability to be assigned long before Tommy Miller entered the picture.

She insisted that there had been a kind of conspiracy, perhaps only an unspoken agreement, between Tommy and Dean, that they would "let her go"; both were weary. And hadn't Tommy given Dean a roll of bills the morning that Mother died? Surely enough for the funeral, and more? (Both Mae and I remember that.) And there was the Edsel; he gave Dean the title. Tommy's generosity to Dean seems just that, but to my grandmother, it seemed a sign of guilt.

It was too soon, my grandmother said. She meant for her. Only she would never have lost patience, would never have given up. Mother had had terrible fevers as a baby. My grandmother recalled sitting out in the shade of a cottonwood tree, dipping water from a bucket to cool Edith's burning skin. Never had Mother called that my grandmother had failed to come, but no matter what she did, it was not enough.

·

LATER IN 1959 Tommy Miller closed his Odessa practice. He had mining interests—tungsten in Canada, gold in Colorado? Eventually he returned to West Texas, opening a practice in Andrews, where many of his patients were indigent. He lived to be quite old, continuing his quiet work. I always thought he changed his life out of grief, proving at last that my mother was right about his goodness and about his love for her.

I saw him once more after Mother's death. It was late in the summer of 1968, that terrible summer of Robert Kennedy's murder, of riots in the streets of our cities and in cities around the world, including Mexico City, where I was from mid-May to early August. I had seen tanks on the broad avenues and had heard terrible rumors that soldiers had shot young students in a confrontation at a preparatory school. This was part of the growing violence between the Mexican government and the protesting students that led, just before the summer Olympics began, to hundreds of deaths and thousands of arrests. I had a lover early in the summer and I didn't take precautions, as if everything that summer was a matter of fate, as if any of what was going on had to do with me.

So when I went to see my aunt in Monahans, Texas, I had missed two periods. She took me to Andrews. Tommy saw me first in his office. He shook my hand warmly and I was embarrassed to have gone to him with my problems and my foolishness. He was patient and neutral and put me at ease. He examined me and said that everything looked fine although he thought I could stand to gain some weight and maybe take vitamins. I dressed and saw him again in the hall. Lying on the exam table, I had had floating thoughts of asking him about my mother, but the nurse had been there, and he had had his hand inside me, and now he looked old and weary and I thought it would be cruel and pointless to bring up the past. He patted my shoulder and said, "You've become a beautiful young woman." I wish I had heard him say he loved her, but I know he did, and I know it was the best kind of love, a deep appreciation of who she was, and who she might have been with a kinder fate.

I CAN'T KNOW FOR SURE how my mother died. If she committed suicide to end her pain, with or without Tommy's help, it would be completely understandable, but I don't think she did. After all I have learned, I believe that my mother died of natural causes: a classic shutdown of the body upon kidney failure. I wish there had been an autopsy to rule out a drug overdose, to save my grandmother decades of bitter grief and my sister some of her anger and the false assumption that she too had "weak kidneys." I wish I had known how to allow Mother her own identity in my memory, but does any child do that, least of all the orphan? I sensed that to the family, and to Dean most of all (he outside the family), Mother seemed obstinately to have lived a life in which everything had been about being sick, as if at least in part she had chosen it. No one wanted to talk about her; no one has ever wanted to talk about anything difficult. (I don't live that way. Things have to get said, even if they are hard.)

And what if it is true that Mother's dreams were too large for the circumstances of her life? That she was foolish to want so much—more children, more education, more opportunity, more wealth and beauty. What if she misjudged the balance of cost and reward in handing me over to the nuns? What if her suffering made her self-centered? What if her whole life was about over-reaching?

So what? She reached for worthy things and she tried to point my sister and me toward a better life. She taught me to look at a larger world. She loved the body and longed to fill the mind and the soul. Her slow death turned out to be the crucible of her maturity. She bore it with courage. The photographs were her testament: Desire dies last of all.

TEN

Daddy traded the Edsel in for a new Chevrolet, a black
Impala with extravagant fins. He pulled up in the driveway and
got out beaming. "Let's take a ride," he said. It was late May, gusty
and dusty and sometimes breakthrough blue. We drove south to
McCamey with the windows down. We ate enchiladas in a tiny
café. Coming back to the car, he tossed me the keys.

He had moved back into the house after the funeral, sleeping in the room with the altar, on which he threw his keys, his
wallet, his battered Mickey Spillane books. I was angry at Father
Lyndale for his grudging attention to Mother at the end, and
angry at God in general, so I packed away the statue of the

Virgin, the rosaries, and holy cards. I didn't go to church, but
Hail Marys sometimes bubbled out of me in the last moments
before I slept.

I thought I could make it up to Daddy for those months of
exile, for widowerhood and all the responsibilities for two kids. I
would love him; I would be there when he came home from work.
Karen was in Kermit, living with our cousins, so there were just the
two of us, but I thought that was temporary, maybe through the
summer while everyone adjusted. She would want to be with
Daddy too. I thought about the night we stopped in a motel on the
way to Wichita Falls for Mother's funeral and he took us bowling
and kept us busy until we were ready to sleep.

I pulled up in the driveway and he said for me to wait while he
opened the garage door. He stepped off onto the grass. I pulled in
too fast and too tight on the right and made a long scratch on the
car door. He yelled for me to stop, waving his arms like crazy, but
then he laughed at how fast his new car had been wounded. I was
in tears, frozen by my humiliation. He helped me out and walked
me to the house with his arm over my shoulders, chuckling and
saying worse things happened all the time. He gave me my own
keys and said to park it in the drive from now on. He said I could
drive when I needed to, but he'd rather I didn't take it to school,
so I only did so when it rained, and I parked in a far corner of the
lot where the traffic was light.

I had been taking the Edsel to school. I don't remember
when I got my license. My sixteenth birthday was in August, and
I assume that's when I would have taken the test, but maybe I
was eligible at fifteen, because I'm sure Daddy wouldn't have let
me drive his new car without insurance and I couldn't have
qualified without a license. He had to have thought about it,

because I drove the car all the way across the state to Corpus Christi in June, trailing behind his Otis truck for twelve straight hours.

·

I HARDLY EVER saw him. A couple times a week at the most, we ate dinner together, usually out. I never knew when he would come home. Often he came and went in the night. The worst time for me was right after school, coming back to the empty house. I turned on the TV in the living room and the radio in the bathroom right away. The door to Mother's bedroom was always shut.

I went to all the speech tournaments and always won something. I put a jar on the dining table to hold my medals. There you go, I would say, tossing one in, knowing she would have been pleased. Other weekends, I stayed at Rita's house on Saturday nights unless I went to my aunt's. Sometimes I spent Sunday afternoon at my speech teacher's house. She had a four-year-old daughter who hugged my knees when I came in. I would take my homework and do it in their kitchen, then watch Ed Sullivan before I went home. My grandmother had gone to Kermit with Aunt Mae after the funeral for a while, then back to Wichita Falls to work. I guess I was the big girl Mother admonished me to be, because no one seemed to think I wasn't all right, alone so much.

When school was out I got right to work on the new debate topic, quickly exhausting the resources of the public library. I wrote to Senator Yarborough, requesting government documents, and telling him about my mother's death, "an unexpected complication of her nephritis." I said I thought he might remember her. He wrote back praising her and offering his sympathy. His office sent two large boxes of documents. In the fall he wrote to offer me an internship in his office after my senior year, something I'm sure I would have wanted to do, but didn't. I assume it was a matter of money, since living expenses would not have been provided. In May, just before graduation, his office sent me a pretty compact.

I tried to get a job, but offices and department stores all told me to come back after my sixteenth birthday. I went to the library and checked out books by the armload and read myself bleary every night. I remember *On the Beach;* it scared me and there was no one I could go to with my fear. One day, coming down the library steps, I met Larry on the walk. He grabbed my arm to stop me. "How could you not call me?" he said. "How could you not tell me Edith died?" I pulled my arm away, I didn't look at him. All I could think about was that last time I saw him, the last day I talked to my mother, when I was mean to her, *and it was all about him.*

"You came to school that day, I heard all about it. Everybody heard. You went all over the school telling teachers and kids your mother was dead, but you didn't come to me!" He didn't stop me when I walked away, but he called after me: "Everybody thinks you're crazy!"

How can I explain what it was like to think and not think about her, both at the same time? I had a noise in my head that roared and the business of my life was to drown it out. The noise said my mother was dead. The noise said she took all her pills and abandoned us. The noise said she didn't give me a chance to say I loved her. When I couldn't stop myself from remembering her, I called up anger to smother the grief. That day I saw Larry, I went home crying and trembling with indignation. I couldn't believe that he had called her Edith. How many afternoons had he visited her, then sped away while I was still in school?

I stormed into the house and stomped to her bedroom. I stood in the hallway staring at her door as if she might come out if she cared enough to do so. With all the furious strength I could muster, I kicked it open. A long crack appeared in the wood and the knob broke into the wall plaster. I pawed through her things, tossing clothes out of her drawers onto the floor. I was looking for her notebooks. I wanted to see what she was thinking before she died. *I wanted her to admit what she had done.* I wanted to read about Larry. Tommy. Pills. I wanted to see my name in her handwriting. Beautiful daughter; big girl; silly little bitch—I didn't care, but *in her writing.* I couldn't find them. I never found them. The photographs were saved, though, because they were in my room. I don't think Daddy ever saw them. He would surely have destroyed them.

That night, alone in the house, I stepped out of the tub and rubbed myself hard with the towel until I felt raw and hot, and then I threw myself face down on the hall floor, my arms flung above my head, pointing toward Mother's room. I wept and I prayed. I asked God to help me remember how to believe. I needed God now more than ever, for myself and for Mother. The next day I called the sisters in Fort Worth and talked to one I hardly knew. She said the sisters had offered Masses for my mother's soul and that they would remember her in their prayers, and me, too. She said that awful thing people say when they mean well, that Mother wasn't suffering anymore, she was with God.

MAYBE I SHOULD say this. Mother was thirty-three when she died. Daddy was thirty-two. I should say, He was there when she died. He got up on her bed and straddled her, bent over her, and cried *Don't do this, Edith!* My grandmother rallied to grab him and pull on his arm, the way she did the day we left her house to live in a housing project with Mexicans. He cried, deep from his belly, and he scooped Karen up from the floor to hold her. I should say, I never heard him say a word of complaint about her. I never heard anyone in her family say a good word about him. I never had a single conversation with him about her, or about anything significant.

. . .

He had to be in Corpus Christi for a week, he said, and he didn't want to leave me by myself. He wondered if I would want to go along? He couldn't take me in the company truck, but I could follow in the Impala, and then we would have a car in Corpus.

I was delirious with excitement. It was a dreadful drive, but we stopped every few hours to get a drink, go to the bathroom, or stretch. I had a radio to keep me company. I could see Daddy checking his rearview mirror; often he stuck his arm out the window and waved. Truckers coming the other way honked and waved to me. Once we stopped to eat at a truck stop where a Halliburton employee motioned Daddy and me over to his booth. They knew each other from the field. Daddy introduced me—"my girl"—and the guy gave me a silly, friendly wink.

We stayed at a motel with a swimming pool and a pleasant patio area with lounge chairs and umbrellas. Our room had two huge beds, and of course a color TV. To me the bathroom was the height of luxury. Every morning I woke up hours after he was gone, and I put on my bathing suit and went out to sunbathe before it was too hot. My bathing suit was two pieces, each with a perky flounce that went all the way around. I didn't go in the water. Carefully, I slathered on suntan lotion and turned myself front and back every fifteen minutes or so, more out of boredom than anything else. After an hour, I pulled on a shirt and shorts and went into the café to eat a sandwich. Back in the room, I turned the air conditioner to freezing, crawled under the covers, and watched soap operas and game shows until I was sleepy. Sometimes I had magazines that had been left out by the pool. I napped, woke sometime after four, put on my bathing suit again, and went out to swim. People checked in and came out by the pool to have a drink or swim. Texans are friendly, and I heard all about their travels and plans. For two nights, four musicians who were performing at a club in town stayed at the motel, and they told me they were going to make it big. I used to know who they were, because they did make some records, but I don't remember anything about them anymore except that they were from Louisiana, and they were young.

I had no real idea what Daddy did when he was working. When he tried to explain, I couldn't understand, but I liked for him to talk to me. My contribution was usually something about what I had seen on television. If he was late and tired we ate at the motel, but usually we took the car to a restaurant in some other part of town. It was like a date.

By the time we got back from dinner, he was ready for bed. "Okay, kiddo," he would say, "I'm calling it a day." I watched TV with the sound down low while he slept. I glanced over at him often; he lay on his back, snoring, his arms flung out from his body. I resolved to learn to cook something really good, something I knew he liked. Chicken and dumplings. Pot roast. I thought of the house. Dust coated every surface. The bathtub had rings upon rings. When I got home I would clean everything. Daddy and I would make a home.

We stopped in Ozona, hardly more than a hamlet, home of a Davy Crockett monument, to fill up the tanks and have something to eat. We were still a couple of hours from home and it was getting dark. Daddy was tired. I said I wanted a little ice cream, and he suggested that he get on the road right away; I could catch up with him. I ordered my ice cream and went to the bathroom. When I got back, he had left. I ate a few bites, too full for more, and stood up to leave. That was when I realized that he had taken my keys off the table along with his.

I knew that, sooner or later, he would realize what he had done. He would notice that he had keys in the ignition and keys in his pocket; he would notice that I hadn't come up behind him even though I could drive faster than he could. I knew that he would come back for me and say he was sorry, and we would laugh about it and remember that time I was stranded in Ozona.

He didn't remember until he got to Odessa, and he didn't come back for me. He went to a truck stop and talked to truckers until he found someone who would be passing me on his way. Hours and hours later, a man came in the café door and asked for me. The lights were turned down by then, the café was closed. The cook had gone home and the mopping was done. The waitress sat with me drinking coffee and showed me photographs of her children. She was young, a Mexican girl with long red fingernails. I told her about Mother and she held my hands. I was embarrassed, but she said I had to understand there were rules about trucks. He couldn't turn around on company time, but he'd get back to me. I said I could wait outside, but she wouldn't leave until I did. She called her baby-sitter to bring her kids, and when they came, we all had pie. The kids ran around and played under the tables. Finally, I got my keys just as she said I would. At least Daddy was home when I got there, waiting for me. I pretended that it was funny, as did he.

The next time he was going to be away four or five days, he made arrangements for me to stay at his boss's house. I protested, but he said they wanted to meet me, the wife was a real nice lady, and it was too long for me to be by myself now that school was out. He took me over there the night before he was leaving and we had supper with them. They had a nice house, the kind of house Mother used to like to visit when a new development opened. She would dress us up as if we were going to church and we'd go out where they'd carved lots into the prairie, built houses all alike, and strung flapping flags to announce that they were open.

We ate dinner. Daddy went home. She showed me to the guest room. It had its own TV and bath, like a motel room.

I lasted two days, tagging around behind her, going to the grocery store, making brownies, taking showers, reading her magazines, watching TV. She didn't say anything about Mother. I told her about debating and she thought that was great. Then I started to cry. Supper was in the oven, her husband was on his way home, and I was wailing like a baby. She put her arms around me and patted my back, and when I didn't stop, she led me to the couch and sat down with me and asked me what she could do. "Poor dear," she kept saying. "Poor dear." I said I wanted to go to my aunt's house, where my little sister was.

When her husband got home, they drove me to Kermit. My aunt was waiting at the door. She swung it wide and said, "Come in here now." She walked them to their car and stood out there talking for a while. I saw them shaking their heads, all three of them.

In a few days my grandmother came out from Wichita Falls. She had taken indefinite leave from the mill and she went back with me to the house. I guess she had talked to Daddy. His stuff was gone. She told me that early in the year, she had applied to the licensed vocational nurse program at Odessa Junior College, a two-year course of study, and that she had received a scholarship and had borrowed some money. She would work part-time at the hospital, too, and with Daddy paying the rent, we would be okay. I pointed out that after I was sixteen I could get a job, but she scoffed and said I'd be too busy with school.

At the end of July, Daddy came by and told us he had rented another house over in the part of town where Rita lived. He said that he couldn't afford the rent on our old house and support himself, too. We had a couple of days to make the move. He said we should take whatever we wanted and then he would clear out the rest. I didn't ask him where he was going. Certainly he wouldn't want to live in a house with my grandmother. Maybe he would go back to Mrs. Doernoff's but I didn't believe he would.

I MISSED THE EDSEL. I never saw another one the whole time we had it. In late April, Rita and I had started going to Tommy's Drive-in to check out the action. The protocol was this: You drove around slowly three or four times, waving to people who caught your eye, then you found a place to park and sat for a while with one of the doors open, if you had room. Rita knew just about everyone. She'd go to a car where a couple were sitting, and lean in the window on the girl's side to talk.

One night we were parked next to Ben Fischel, who was by

himself. A senior, he was tall, dark, and handsome. He was also a Jew, just about the most exotic person I could imagine. He dated beautiful, popular girls, but he didn't go steady. He had been the homecoming queen's escort in the fall. (Rita filled me in on this in one minute flat.) She talked to him a little, and then he got out and came around to my side and opened the door. He said, "Scoot over, let me look at this car." He said he'd always wanted to drive one. The next thing I knew, the three of us were taking a ride.

The next time I saw him at the drive-in, he came over and said something to Rita, who got out and went to talk to someone in another car. In a few minutes she came back and said she needed to go home. I said sure, and started the car. As I pulled out, Ben followed me. I dropped Rita off and he came and said I should leave my car and go for a ride in his. My heart was thumping, but I did want to do just that. I couldn't leave the car at Rita's, though, her mother would want to know why, so I had him follow me back to my house. I told him to wait a minute, and I went inside and turned on some lights so I wouldn't have to come back to a dark house, and I ran a brush through my hair, rinsed out my mouth, and went outside to Ben's car.

He reminded me of Larry, in a way. He had that same slow, sarcastic, brooding, observing manner, though I don't think he was as nice as Larry. He seemed to feel superior, and I thought he was. I said, "What do you want to do?" and he laughed. I was embarrassed, shy, and scared, but I was also thrilled. I didn't care what he wanted to do.

He took me out of town to a side road and parked the car. He left the radio on. I was sitting close to him and he put his arm on the seat behind me and we talked a while. He asked me about my mother; I said she had died recently and I didn't like to talk about it. He asked me about my father, and I said he was out on a job until late. His father was a dentist, and he was going to study dentistry, too. That about covered it. He started kissing me. I wasn't wearing a padded bra, and I was glad, although when he undid the one I was wearing and began fondling me, I couldn't relax, thinking how little I was, how he must be thinking that. I pulled away and said, "I don't really like that so much, and I don't see why you would." I was pleased with myself because I thought I sounded confident.

He laughed again, sat back, and asked me what I did like. I said I didn't know. Then I laughed too. It was a silly thing to say. I said I didn't know what he thought, but I didn't—you know—I didn't do *that*.

"How about," he said, "if I promise you that we won't do *that*? If I promise I won't make you do anything? I'll just help you find out what you like."

"Okay," I said. I don't know how he kept a straight face.

He caressed me for a long time, and then he slid his hand up under my skirt, along my thighs. He traced the edge of my panties while I clamped my teeth to keep from squealing with pleasure. He slipped his finger under the elastic and I writhed, then pulled away.

He didn't push me past that. He sat back against his window, looked at me with a big satisfied grin, and said, "There's one thing you like, wouldn't you say?" I smiled, but I couldn't look at him.

I went with him half a dozen times, always meeting him at the drive-in. I went during the week, alone, looking for him. He gave me the same slow, sly once-over, maybe pretended he was leaving, or went off to talk to someone, but then he started his car and followed me home. Once he asked me where my dad was all the time, and I said in the oil field.

He never hurried. He found something to talk about, maybe a movie one of us had seen, or an election campaign at school. Then he would cock his head, as if to say, shall we get on with it? Each time he was a little more aggressive, until his finger was inside me. The last time we went out on our drive, he asked me if I would have intercourse—he used the word, which I had never heard—and I said I couldn't. He didn't press the matter. I understood that that was the end of the line with him, and I didn't go to Tommy's anymore. I told Rita that it embarrassed me to go on the weekend with her, when everyone else had a date. I felt sorry for what I had missed by not going on with him, but I knew he didn't care about me and that I would have been sorry. It was all too dispassionate; I wanted to be swept away. I did think I had made some kind of progress, though.

In my bed, I tried to do what he had done, but it wasn't the same. And when I did have intercourse, a long time after, I lost that thrill of expectation, the terrible, wonderful demand of my body for *more*. When you know what will happen next, and you know you will have it happen, you lose innocence and your patience, and you can never get them back.

I saw him once at school in the hall. He raised his hand to wave; he wiggled his middle finger and laughed as he passed by. I didn't get the feeling that he was being mean.

DURING MY SENIOR YEAR, once in a while my grandmother and I went to Wichita Falls on a Saturday so that she could check on her house. I went to Mass the next morning at Saint Michael's. I thought of it as Mother's church. Sitting in a pew maybe a third of the way from the back, I felt a tormenting nostalgia. I closed my eyes and for a flicker of a moment I was a little girl again in a pretty dress with white gloves sitting beside my mama; then it was that terrible Wednesday after Easter when we prayed her funeral Mass.

One Sunday as I was coming out of church I met Father Daly and he invited me to the rectory for a cup of coffee. He asked me how I was doing, and of course I burst into tears. I told him that I hadn't been going to Mass. Everything poured out: how Mother had stopped going, and how the priest had disliked her. How my family was broken up. I said that I didn't remember how to pray, that I didn't know if I believed anything anymore. I remember saying, "I tried so hard, and it didn't do any good."

He was a beautiful, patient man. He sat across from me. He took both my hands in his. He said that God would be patient with me and that I must be patient with God. I should simply do the best I could, and that I should never worry about my mother. She had been an extraordinary person, and now she was at peace. It all sounded fine coming from him. I didn't want to leave him. I wanted to crawl up on his lap and put my arms around his neck like a little girl.

DADDY HAD BEEN SEEING a Jewish woman from Canada. Her name was Phyllis Greene; she had changed her surname from Greenberg. She was a lawyer's secretary. She had met an Odessa attorney who was in Edmonton for some reason, and she had come to Odessa on a whim to work for him, desperate to get away from her parents. She had been living with them after a brief marriage. They were raising her son.

She was unlike any woman I had ever seen. She dyed her hair red and wore it in a long pageboy. She had large breasts and hips and cinched her waist in tight. She wore big skirts with flouncy under-skirts, and high sandal heels. She spoke in a high, bright voice.

I met her around the time of my high-school graduation. She and Daddy were married by then. They were living in a nice apartment complex. There was a pool just out from their front door. I was jealous. Daddy had invited me over to have supper with them—we would go out, Phyllis didn't like to cook—but first they wanted to give me my graduation gift. I don't remember what it was, some piece of jewelry that I never wore. It was evening and we sat poolside. I could see that Daddy was proud of her and anx-ious for me to like her. I was sullen, unable to summon the cour-tesy the situation called for. Daddy said he would go call for a reservation. We were going to a nice steak house, he said.

As soon as he left us, Phyllis tapped me on the knee and said, "Please look at me while I talk to you." Shocked, I did. She seemed to be holding her eyebrows up high, making her look a little drunk.

She said, "It wasn't my idea to get married, but Richard said he didn't want a girlfriend, he wanted a wife. A home. He said he hadn't had either in a long time."

Richard? His name was Richard Dean, always Dean, and sud-denly, for her, he was *Richard?*

Tears sprang to my eyes. I stared hard at her.

"I knew there were you two girls, and I accepted that. And I told him he should keep treating you like his own child, even though you're not. He had to give your grandmother money for rent while you were still in school. With that money, we could have bought some furniture instead of renting the crap we've got, but I told him, 'We'll wait.'"

She paused, as if she expected me to respond, but what could I say? I was thinking, *He told her and he never told me.* I took a series of noisy gulps, jerking my head forward, before I got control. I stared at my pale, skinny knees, then covered them with my palms.

She went on and on. There was a droning sound in my head, but her high, sure voice cut through it.

"Now you're not going to be in high school anymore, you can get a job just like the rest of us, so don't push it. Your mother's gone and most girls your age go to work until they get married and have families. I don't see the point of college, to tell you the truth, but Richard says you want to go. You made good grades and you've got ideas about yourself. So here is how it is. We're not going to keep on supporting your grandmother. And we're not going to keep on supporting you. If you insist on going to college, you can go right here at the junior college, and you can live with us. It won't cost very much to feed you, and Richard says you have a scholarship for tuition and books. I want you to know that this isn't something Richard is pushing on me. He wouldn't do anything I didn't want him to do. But I'll meet you halfway because he's the only father you've known and evidently the real one hasn't ever been in the picture. Just remember you aren't a child anymore and you better not act like one with me because I won't put up with it. And remember I'm his wife and our marriage comes first."

Daddy came out and Phyllis smiled up at him and said that we had had a little talk and now we had an understanding. There was something in the way they looked at each other that shut me out at the same time that it sent me a message. I was sure that he had told her, *She might as well hear it now as later.* What I despised was the idea of them talking about me. About his not-daughter. Maybe he had said, *poor kid,* and Phyllis jumped up to say, *I can tell her.*

I was shocked, as if I had reached for the mashed potatoes and had my hand cut off, but it did not occur to me that she might be lying. It was too essential a fact, and she was too confident for it not to be true. And it explained things. Why my grandmother was so sure that Daddy's family wouldn't like me. Why my grandmother favored me. Why my sister and I looked so different. It drove me crazy to think of all the adults keeping this secret from me my whole life. It made me feel stupid, like someone with something written on her forehead that everyone else can read.

"You hungry, kiddo?" Daddy said to the air between Phyllis and me. He was being cheery and everything about him said, *Don't let's carry this any further.*

I stood up and said I wasn't feeling well, I wanted to go home and not go to the steak house after all. I sat in the back seat of the car crying and hiccuping while Phyllis told Daddy a joke from the office and he laughed with that big *har har* heartiness of his.

They drove me to my house and let me out. I had stopped crying but my grandmother could see my swollen eyes. She said, "You don't have to see them. He won't care." She was going to have her heart broken. She thought he was going to be out of our lives, and instead he was going to take me out of hers.

I DIDN'T GET UP the nerve to ask her about my "real" father until I was twenty. She showed me a birth certificate that said, "Albert Berry." She said that Albert was a sweet boy who had lived in their Gallup, New Mexico, neighborhood until he joined the Navy, about the same time my grandmother got her factory job in

Wichita Falls and moved with her kids. He had let Edith use his name, but they had just been friends; he wasn't the father. She said she didn't know who was. In fact, Mother had so "used his name" that she had pretended to be married to him, then pretended to be divorced; I have letters addressed to "Mrs. Edith Berry" from relatives. Even Albert addressed letters to Edith Berry! But when he came to Wichita Falls after the war, she wouldn't see him, and Aunt Mae took him around for two days, and then he went away. From the letters I learned that he was in San Diego when Mother went to California in 1943. I think she must have gone to marry him, but he shipped out too soon, so she just said that they married and came home.

My illegitimacy and my mother's deception must have been a source of both her vulnerability and her power over my grandmother and of constant tension about me through my childhood. Mother needed and loved Frieda, but it is hard to depend on someone when you want to be an adult, and even harder when your own child has always lived with your mother. Except for less than a year in Ohio, from the day I was born until I was nine years old, I was as much Frieda's child as Edith's. Frieda lived to be seventy-seven, dying just after I turned forty, and all the tears I wasn't able to shed when Mother died were like a flood behind a flood, as if I lost them both at the same time.

AT THE END of the summer, I moved in with Daddy and Phyllis. I took twenty-one credits a term and worked part-time as a department-store clerk. Most of my life revolved around speech and drama. The following August, I moved to Austin.

I never was in a room alone with Daddy again. Once, when I was determined to talk to him about the possibility of transferring to the Catholic college outside Dallas, I set my alarm so that I would wake up when he did. I was afraid he would brush me off if I tried to catch him as he left. I knew that he would go out to Johnny's Café for coffee and donuts, and I hurriedly walked there to meet him. In front of other people, he would have to hear me out. It was to no good; all he said was that it was up to Phyllis, she was the "manager."

We never spoke about what Phyllis had told me. Partly I was sure that we were held together by a fragile thread now, and as long as we ignored the uncovered knowledge, the thread wouldn't snap. Partly I couldn't bear to hear him brush it off as inconsequential: *Ho ho, now don't you worry about that.* And after a while I came to like the idea that I was my mother's child alone, as if I had sprung from her head like a mythical creature.

I saw Dean (as I now think of him) for the last time when I was twenty-three. I was passing through town with an Italian boyfriend and we stopped at his insistence. My boyfriend's name was Richard, too, but he liked to be called Dick. I had been living with him in Chicago for about a year. Daddy and Phyllis liked him. He was forty years old, a successful attorney, caustic, patronizing to me. We drove to Hobbs, New Mexico, for dinner and dancing at a new motel and spent the night there. We took two cars so that Dick and I could go on the next morning. At dinner, Phyllis bragged that she had taught Dean (*Richard!*) to dance, and now he was expert. Dean, in turn, bragged that she had been a ballroom-dancing champion in Canada and had participated in a competition in Las Vegas. I was not impressed.

They danced smoothly while we watched, and then Dick and

I danced, less expertly. Then we switched partners. It was very awkward for me, dancing with Dean, but he seemed to be concentrating on his technique, breathing hard through his mouth, and neither of us said anything. After a few drinks, Dick started teasing me for their benefit, telling anecdotes about me in a way that emphasized the carelessness of my youth, saying things that made Dean and Phyllis laugh at me. I had gone to Rome with him to visit his father, a retired diplomat, and his stepmother had made a big show of cooling my Cokes with their wine in a silver ice bucket; telling it now was cruel riposte. I didn't try to explain to him how much he embarrassed and hurt me. I knew that all I had to do was leave him, and I did.

·ELEVEN·

So this is love! This pounding heart, the gush to the head when he enters the room, the struggle to find perfect words for feelings.

His name was Richard, too. He signed things "R.E." in his tiny, tight writing, a sign, I should have recognized, of his crabbed heart. He was in his second year at Odessa Junior College and he was the big fish: champion tennis player, student council president, voted Mr. Odessa College. Everyone admired him but I don't think he had real friends except his tennis partner. He was too intense, an alien, like me; how did we land on this planet in West Texas, when there were grand cities where you were free to be your truest self?

That was the way we talked. His father was a Jew from New

York who married his mother, a nurse from West Texas, during World War II when she was working in the east. They had their problems, he said; he lived a separate life. He took me to his house, almost as shabby as the one my grandmother and I had been living in until I moved into Daddy's apartment. He had a large room with an entrance from the alley and its own bathroom, and he had made that his lair, with a lock on the door to the kitchen. We sat in the near dark with a single lamp and told each other everything we had ever read. He gave me Henry Miller and I gave him Robinson Jeffers. I showed him some of my poems and I watched him read them. He had a small mouth and as he read, he pursed it until it looked like an inverted beak. He didn't touch me. Once he said, "I think these things, too, but I can't find words the way you do." The poems were overblown, but each hit home with an adolescent girl's idea of thrust. One example: *I've seen ice / I know how cold the cold can be / I know fires are kindled just to die. / I've watched storms pass over and / I've touched stone where her body lies. / I can't remember what life was like / before I put cross and marker / over my hope* (dated 12/59).

Richard was tormented, even then. His stewing-and-ruing was the engine that kept him moving and put off sparks we thought were charisma. He was golden but he knew it wouldn't last. He was going to ruin his life and he didn't know how to not let that happen. He liked to think he was protecting me from his melancholy fate, and maybe he was.

We were in the school play, *The Heiress*, based on the Henry James novel *Washington Square*. He was cast as Morris Townsend, rake and suitor of a plain-Jane heiress. I couldn't imagine why I didn't get the lead instead of sweet Marlee, who was, I thought, too robust for the part. I played a busybody friend of the family. Rita had a little part, too.

I was bold about asking for rides. Phyllis would pick me up if I called, but she wouldn't want to. Richard lived not far from me, and soon it fell to him to get me home. The first couple of times we talked with the motor running, then we parked at the curb. By the second week we were going to his room. One windy night we drove around and finally parked by the high-school football field. I was cold, and he raised his arm to take me under it, then kissed me for the first time.

The front seat was cramped and we were all limbs. There was a false start, my tears, but I ended up beneath him, my panties down. He said, *Are you sure?* And I cried out, *Oh yes!* So happy, *it was finally happening,* and with someone I loved. But when he fumbled and pressed against me, I was scared and I said *Ow,* and he was off me in a second, growling that I should have told him I was a virgin.

He got out of the car and walked onto the field. I regained my composure and chased after him. The wind was up and I could see us the way you saw Natalie Wood and James Dean at the side of the cliff where her boyfriend has died playing chicken with his car. Richard shoved me away, told me to get back in the car, and in a short while he drove me home.

He avoided me at rehearsal, but others gave me rides. I called him at home one night after rehearsal, infuriating him. His folks were sleeping. You don't call, he said. Girls don't call.

OF COURSE I wrote about it:

He ran his hand soothingly along her leg, waiting for her sobs to stop. The dry grass chafed his arm. Her skin was bumpy with the cold. She had come to him across the field, crying for him. "I'm sorry!" she said again and again. "I was so confused, afraid, I was afraid to say I love you! But when you walked away, I couldn't stand it. Come back, I'll do anything if only you won't run away from me ever again." They walked to the car. She slid onto the seat; he almost laughed as she positioned herself so primly, feet on the floor, hands in her lap. "I want you," he said. "If we start again I'm going to finish. You have to say yes before I'll even kiss you." He ran his hand down the pink stripe of her shirtwaist. He slipped the dress off her shoulders. He felt her stiffen as he unclasped her bra, but she didn't move. Her little breasts were perfectly formed, so delicate. Slowly, he helped her remove her underwear. He dismissed her awkward tension, her near apathy, as virgin ignorance, but when he lay on her, he felt her chest heaving, and he gritted his teeth as she burst into anguished cries" (dated 10/60).

It went on for twenty pages. I gave it to Rita to read.

"That bastard," she said. "He nearly nailed you."

I wrote a poem and slipped it through his car window onto the seat: *He'll come, and leap your heart / to seek him in the night. / He'll touch, / and clasp his fingers / warm around your soul. / He'll bring you flowers / hot with scent / and leave you / when they die.*

Everything about the play was torturous now. I was so tense in rehearsals and performance that my stomach cramped, but I wept when the show closed. We had no classes in common; I hardly ever saw him. I wanted to tell him, *Try, try again,* but I didn't have the chance. Then we had a meeting about an upcoming tournament. He was doing a scene from the play and I was debating. I said "Hi" and he glared at me, then sat where I couldn't see his face. When the meeting was over, he came up behind me and touched my shoulder. He had my poem in his hand, and he shook it at me. "Don't give me this shit!" he said. "You're not old enough to write poems about love!" That ultimate insult: *little girl.*

One morning I was in the student union, sitting with a pretty girl from my English class, a girl named Karen, like my sister. I was pleased to be at a table with her. She seemed so sophisticated. We were talking about Richard; I was close to telling her about trying to make love with him. She had known him all her life. She said he had always been special, and he had always been "two inches off the mark." I had no idea what that meant. Because of what was in my mind (my panties on his car floor, my knees up in the moon-light) I was hearing it as a literal description. Suddenly it seemed funny and I laughed. At that moment, Karen raised her arm and waved at someone coming into the union from outdoors.

It was a girl named Cookie. She had been a high-school cheer-leader in Midland, and she carried herself with verve and confi-dence even though she wasn't especially good in school. She had a broad face and wide-set eyes, the kind of beauty that Jackie Kennedy would make so public in another year, but in Odessa in the fall of 1960, Cookie was just odd, in her effervescent way. She came to our table, gave me a brisk nod and leaned over to show Karen the fat athletic ring that dangled on a chain around her neck. Karen's eyes widened with girlish glee: *"He didn't!"*

Cookie pulled up a chair and sat down. "He gave it to me last night. I love him so much!"

Beyond her I saw Richard coming in the door. He stopped, caught in the bright sunshine, and held his hand up to his eyes, scanning the room. Then Karen saw him and waved and he came toward our table in long strides, smiling. Karen punched Cookie's arm, Cookie turned and saw him, stood up as he approached the table, and locked her arm in his.

I fled the table and the room, the day's classes, and my high hopes for R.E. and me.

I WANTED TO TALK to someone, and there was no one who would understand. Rita had already told me that Richard was a "stuck-up" and a "psycho." Every girl who knew him said he was weird but they all admired him anyway. Rita had said, "He'll push all your buttons and make you cry," and she was so right, I wouldn't talk to her until Christmas.

Phyllis came home from work and found me red-eyed and list-less on the couch. I was trying to read one of her Barbara Cartland novels, some kind of abnegation. She was carrying a sack of gro-ceries. I knew that meant that Daddy was coming home in time for supper and she was making one of her dinners: spicy spaghetti, roast chicken smothered in onions, or beef stroganoff. She set the sack down and went to her room to change into a flowing loose dress, what we called a muu-muu. She pulled her hair into a pony-tail. She only cooked a few times a month, and she made a huge production of it to celebrate that *Richard* was home. Usually, they went out; if he was working, she didn't eat at all, the better to cut some calories. One day a week she fasted completely except for juice and coffee. There was never food in the house except for these special occasions. I ate lunch at school, and at night, a candy bar. To be fair, she had told me she would buy food if I made a list, but it was too nerve-wracking to try to cook something for myself in front of her.

She emptied the sack and began chopping green pepper, a sign it was spaghetti, the only one of her dishes I liked. She worked for ten minutes or so and then she said brightly, "You might as well tell me what's going on. It isn't good to sit around moping. Either you can do something about it, or you can get it off your chest and move on. I'm all ears, believe me. I have no idea what you do when you leave this house. So go on and tell me. It's about a boy, isn't it?" She put her knife down, leaned her elbows on the counter, and gave me a warm smile. "All of us go through it, sweetheart, really, all of us." It was the nicest she had ever been.

At that, I began to cry in earnest and then to talk. I told her about Richard, how perfect he was for me, how talented and smart and artistic. He wanted to be a lawyer and a writer and an actor and he wanted to leave Texas. He read poetry and novels and he said that I was like a piece of his soul. I didn't say anything about the night by the football field.

I wanted to talk about Richard, of course, but just as much, I wanted to please her. To interest her. I had been living with her for two months and we had never done more than exchange a few words. So, once I had run out of all else I could think to say, I added, "And Phyllis, he's Jewish!" I thought she would find that wonderful. I knew absolutely nothing about Jews or prejudice against them. In Odessa, you were white, black, or brown.

By then I could smell peppers and onions and I was hungry. "That smells good," I told her.

She said, "Go wash your face and forget about Richard. If he liked you so much, he wouldn't humiliate you in front of everyone at school. Besides, you don't know about Jewish boys. He'll use a girl and toss her aside until he meets the one he wants, and then he'll treat her like a princess. A nice, rich Jewish girl. You're lucky it's this Cookie girl and not you."

"But there aren't rich Jewish girls in Odessa!" I was guessing.

"Of course not. Didn't you say he was going to move away?" Plop. She emptied a big can of tomatoes into her electric skillet.

"Besides, you are much too young to be in love. You don't know the first thing about it. If you want sex you have to wait a few years until you aren't a little girl and a grown-up man will be attracted to you. And believe me, you want a man, not a boy, someone who will know how to do more than get off. If you're really lucky, and you grow up a whole lot, you might meet someone as sexy as Richard." Her smile again. "*My* Richard." She turned her back on me to do something at the counter, and I went to my room.

A little later she came to say that she would make an appointment for me with her beautician. "It's time to get rid of that bleached look. And you should cut it. You haven't got the face to carry a pageboy. And if you are going to screw, you better let me get you a doctor's appointment, too."

I said I didn't plan to *do that*.

"There's no point in having you repeat history, is there?"

"Go away," I said.

"Watch how you talk to me. Richard won't put up with your sass."

I didn't eat. That night, I heard them in their bedroom, as I did every night that Daddy was home. Their low voices rumbling, her high giggles, and then the bed squeaking rhythmically under their bulk, the sound soon joined by her shrill cries and his grunts. I put my pillow over my head and cried, my nose straight down into the mattress, and when I was all cried out, I moved to a dry spot.

I did go to her beautician, though. She matched my roots and cut my hair into a flattering bob, and taught me how to set it and comb it out. It was nice, but I thought of it as Phyllis's hairdo, and when I moved to Austin, I bleached my hair white.

·

NO ONE asked me out. I have a yearbook here from that year, and as I sit and look through it, I see many boys I remember as nice, kids from my classes, or from debate or the plays, but none of them could have been my boyfriend. I had too many emotional needs. I wanted to be transported. I might as well have been wearing spikes.

School was easy, even with so many subjects, except for biology, taught by my old chemistry teacher, Mrs. Filleman. I threw myself into debate, partnering again with Lynelle Wood. We had won the state AAAA high-school championship, and we did well on the junior-college circuit. I hung out with Rita, but in her own way, she was moving away from me; she was maturing faster. College didn't suit her. Academics were hard for her, and she had other skills. She had been dancing since she was a little girl and though she couldn't hope to perform professionally, because she had a short, stocky body, she had been apprenticing as a teacher for years. Now she looked around her and realized that there were as many outlying towns as she could count that had no dance teachers. She set up a circuit, and within the year, she was making real money and she was too busy for me.

I wrote dozens of bad poems and when I had a sheaf of five or six that I liked, I would type them up and give them to Richard. I would shove them into his car through the window—it was never rolled up all the way. I'd give them to Karen to give to him. I'd mail them to him. Over Christmas he called me one night and we talked for at least an hour. He said that he missed me, but he knew it was the right thing for me to stay away from him. Such arrogance! And I bit into it like caramel. "I'd just bring you down," he said. "I'm no good for you."

"Are you good for Cookie?"

He laughed. "You don't know anything about that."

I knew it was because I was a virgin. I begged him to give me another chance.

"No. We're so lucky that we stopped. I'd have only hurt you. We'd get too deep with one another, and in the end you'd see you can't depend on me for anything. You need to leave me alone. Move on. Really, you need to grow up."

A few days later I called his house. His mother answered and I left a message. I think he had his own phone but he didn't give the number out. He called me late one night soon after and told me in a low, angry tone, that I was never, ever to call him. I spent the rest of the vacation moping at Aunt Mae's house, telling myself that even if he changed his mind and called me, *I wasn't home*.

SECOND SEMESTER, Lili came to town. She had graduated in Richard's Odessa High School class and had been working in Las Vegas as a showgirl. After a car accident she couldn't wear the big headdresses and she came home to start college. She didn't have the slightest interest in school, and she quit going at the end of the semester, but she had an effect on all of us in theater and speech, as if she had turned up the lights. She was loud and energetic, cheerful and vulgar and generous. The spring play was Sophocles' *Electra,* set in the Trojan War. Lili was Clytemnestra, who betrayed her husband, Agamemnon, and I played one of her daughters. She gave me rides, and soon we were spending a lot of time together. (It was warm enough to use the apartment pool.) I told her I had heard that she had slept with just about everyone in high school and she laughed. She said if she had known how many poor guys were dying for want of sex, she would have been happy to have taken care of them all, but in fact her reputation was mostly bluff. She had preferred the company of her many girlfriends. One guy she had fucked, though, was Richard. (This was the first time I had ever heard the word *fuck* spoken.)

"He's poison," she told me. "Poison. He gets under your skin and makes you sick. You stay clear."

I told her about what had happened with Richard—my timidity and confusion and his gruff rejection of me—and that I never again wanted to be in that awkward awful position. "That just proves my point!" she shrieked, but I insisted that it wasn't Richard I cared about now, it was me. I wanted to be grown-up, I wanted to make my own decisions. *I wanted to be a woman.* I asked her if she could help me find someone I could "lose my virginity" with, someone who would be nice to me and wouldn't talk about me.

"Of course!" she said. "Oh, you little monkey." She rubbed her hands together. "Let's see. There's Charles, but he doesn't know a damned thing. Eddie D., he's cute and he'd be game—"

I said no, I'd had a class with him, he was too big a smart-ass.

She snapped her fingers. She knew just who would do. There was a party Saturday night and I'd go with her. It was at the house of a friend of hers who wasn't in school, Kevin. He was throwing it before he went off to the Army. She promised to talk to him. That night, she called to say she'd pick me up. "Wear something pretty. Something easy to get out of."

It was just that simple. Kevin was glad to oblige. I remember very little about the night. There were a lot of people at the party and I knew only a few of them. Most were older, working. There was a keg and I drank beer. I'm not a drinker. I don't like the taste of liquor; I feel alcohol quickly and get sick, so I don't think I had more than a couple of glasses over the evening, but it was enough to keep me from being too nervous. There were some couples, of course, but most of the guests were singles and friends, so I danced with four or five guys and enjoyed myself. Lili was the last to leave, except for me, of course.

Kevin was nice enough, an okay-looking, not especially smart guy I never would have gone out with on my own. He put music on (Del Shannon) and he kept asking me if I was sure. *He* told *me,* "I never did anything like this before," and we both laughed and that broke the ice. I had a moment when I wished I hadn't thought up such a thing to do, but I told myself it was a way to lose my naïveté. I closed my eyes and gripped his shoulders and waited for it to be over. It was clumsy but it didn't hurt. I thought about telling Richard that he was the one who got me past the pain, that maybe he was the first, after all.

I WAS SCARED, coming into the apartment at three in the morning. The next day Phyllis came home and gave me a slip of paper. It was an appointment slip with a gynecologist. She didn't say anything except, "They'll bill me."

I was embarrassed. The doctor asked me what birth control I was using. I remembered Kevin's rubber, but I couldn't say the word. I shrugged. The doctor wrote out a prescription for birth control pills and told me sternly not to skip any. That evening, when Phyllis got home, she gave me this look, her eyebrows up high, a question.

I nodded.

"You're welcome," she said. "Maybe the pills will help your acne."

·

AFTER I WENT to live in Austin, Phyllis wrote me a series of letters advising me about sex. She said again that what I needed was
an older, experienced man, someone who was patient, with a sense
of humor and a true passion for women. My face burned, reading
her words, because I knew that she was describing Daddy, showing off her possession of him. She wrote other things, using frank,
sometimes vulgar language, attempting, I suppose, to be cozy and
forthright. I dismissed those letters easily enough.

What I couldn't dismiss was how they made me ache for the
sound of my mother's voice. What would she tell me now? What
cautions would she urge on me? Maybe she would say, *Watch your
heart, my darling. And be careful in the dark.*

I HAD TO DECIDE for myself about boys: Romance was a dead
end but I thought sex would be fine. I thought maybe I could be
good at it and I thought that sex might be the way to find someone
I could talk to, the thing I really wanted. I was lonely. I was going
to a university in a great college town where there were hundreds
of parties every month and someone would like me. I sometimes
moped about Richard, but mostly I was sunny about my prospects.
I was a good dancer. One of my roommates was a licensed beautician, and she was glad to bleach my hair. It wasn't really me, but
it sure wasn't Phyllis, either.

The trouble was I really didn't have any way to meet anybody.
Most of those parties were fraternity-sorority mixers. I didn't

belong to any clubs. I lived in the back carriage house of a big boardinghouse in one of four rooms, each with four girls. Next door there was a similar arrangement for boys, and the two groups became friends. During the evenings, the house owners would unlock the gate into the alley, and the boys could come into the courtyard and hang around. Sometimes a group of us went to the movies or out to eat on Saturday night. One by one, pairs formed. There was one boy I liked a lot, Bobby, but he fell for a New Jersey girl and began dating her. Bobby and I became close friends anyway and have kept in touch ever since, but for all his good feelings toward me, it did nothing for my Saturday nights.

So I asked a couple of the girls in the house to see if their boyfriends knew anyone who might want to double. They paid more for their rooms, wore great clothes, and had dates every Friday and Saturday, so I knew they would come through eventually, and the girls were flattered. Sure, they said.

Right away boys started calling. I heard you're a good dancer. Want to go to a party, and so on. They all ran together, those boys, too dull for words, but I didn't lose my optimism. People have to click, I thought; I certainly wasn't looking for another R.E.

One Saturday in late October I walked over to the 7-11 to get some Cokes. I was at the register when a boy tapped me on the shoulder and said, "Glad to see you on your feet."

I turned to see who it was saying something so dumb, and instantly I remembered how we knew one another. During registration, which took place in ninety-degree weather with high humidity, I had had to wait outside on the steps for two hours, and just before my group was due to go into the building for registration, I passed out and fell straight back into the arms of two guys behind me. People started fanning me, someone got a cup of water, and in no time I was on my way. Later I wished we had exchanged names.

Now there they were, both of them. They had fake IDs to buy beer. There was a football game on TV that afternoon, the University of Texas against I don't know what team. We chatted for a moment and they invited me to come home with them to watch the game. They were going to order pizza. "There's not going to be a Texan on the streets, you know!" they said.

I had not been to a game. As a student, I was able to draw tickets and then turn around and sell them—not legal, but done widely, and a very nice supplement to my small income as a tutor in the speech lab. I told them I would come if they would explain a few things about football first, and they agreed. Off we went merrily on what had to be a classic Austin fall afternoon, doing just what thousands of students were doing all over the city.

I got drunk for the very first time. They had two cases of beer and they kept throwing them back. I could only sip, but I did so steadily, mostly to combat my utter boredom. By the time the pizza arrived, it smelled disgusting to me. I made it through halftime and then I began to feel sick. I said the room was going 'round and 'round. One of the guys pointed to a door and said, "Pick either bed and go lay down until you feel better. It's cool." So I did.

There was an air-conditioner in the bedroom, and heavy shades. In the cool dark, I sat on the edge of the messy, unmade bed for what seemed like a long time, too sick to lie down. I peed and I threw up, something I later was sorry for though it made me feel better at the time. I was still too drunk to do anything but go to sleep.

This has to be the most ordinary of tales. On that same day it was probably happening to at least ten other girls in Austin, and hundreds on campuses around the country. I was drunk and dumb and I went to sleep. The game ended. The boys were drunk and decided they were horny; after all, there was a girl in their bedroom. A third guy had turned up, meanwhile

I woke to the sensation of suffocation. I was naked except for my bobby socks. One of the boys was on me, then in me. I moaned, *No!* but I had no strength. I didn't really feel much with the first boy, but the second one hurt me. I was dry and tight and scared. He was big, and maybe he was more drunk, or less drunk than the first boy, and he kept at it a long time. He held himself up with his hands flattened on my breasts, leaning so hard against them I thought they might tear away. I cried and begged him to stop but my protests were feeble. I tried to gag but I couldn't even do that. I stopped pushing and striking him and threw my arms straight out at my sides, off the bed. One hand slid across the crotch of another boy and he giggled and hopped back. I tasted the sour beer again, I remembered where I sat on the couch when I first entered the apartment, I imagined myself leaving before anyone scored—and then the big boy was done with me.

I heard the third boy say, "There's something I always wanted to do." More talk, and some guffaws. Someone spitting. I remember them shoving me and turning me over, pulling me up from behind and spreading my legs apart; and suddenly there was a pain unlike anything I had ever felt in my life, a searing, tearing pain that went up the center of my body and came out in my hoarse cries and pleas. One of the other boys wanted to try it, too. It was the big boy. He hooted and laughed at the surprise of the ride. I thought I was screaming, but no sound came out. Then there was silence, and dark.

I lay there for hours, in and out of consciousness. When I finally got up, the apartment was dark. I turned on the light, a dim bulb overhead. My skirt and panties were on the floor. I had bled on the sheets. I dabbed at myself with a towel in their filthy bathroom and dressed, then I stumbled out onto the street. I felt as if I had been turned inside out. I walked home slowly in the dark, crying. I passed hordes of drunk college boys and I stepped off the walks to make way for them, sometimes backing into darkness behind trees.

In my room, I showered and scrubbed my body hard except for those parts that were horribly abraded. I sat on the floor of the shower and let tepid water run on me. I dried by touching myself gently with a tee shirt over and over, then I put Vaseline on the outside of my vagina. I couldn't bear to touch myself on the other places. I took five or six aspirin and went to bed.

There were no words in my head. I was as empty of language as a feral child. My roommates came in at curfew and asked me if I was sick, if I needed anything, and I said I just wanted to sleep. I lay half-awake all night, kept awake by the burning pain, knowing that everything had changed for me. Who had I thought I was?

And it came to me that I was my mother. Something like this had happened to her all those years ago, something she could never tell anyone, not even her own mother, because it was too shameful to be so vulnerable and so stupid. She had married Daddy because he was a gentle person. Ever after, she had wanted something more, something better, because the core of her was gone. Somebody had hurt her when she was younger than I was, and from that, came me.

You can't make your life into something you have dreamed about. It comes to you. Whether you wait for it by the window or you go out looking, life comes to you as it will and it gives you your chance at sainthood or happiness or it shorts you and you have to make the best of what you've got. I knew that what had happened was my fault, but what I felt was not guilt and not quite shame. It was the simple absence of pride. Those boys gave my name away, and we had so many ugly calls we had to change the phone number to an unlisted one. I told my roommates that I didn't know who was doing it, or why, but they didn't believe me.

It never occurred to me to tell someone in authority what had happened, and I didn't go to a doctor then. It took a long time for the abrasions and tears to heal, and some damage had to be repaired much later, but I went back to classes after a few days. I didn't date again until after the Christmas holidays, and I did so out of stubbornness. In Odessa, Daddy told me that Phyllis's son was coming from Canada to live with them, and Karen; there wasn't room for me. They'd like to see me, of course, he said; I could drive over from Aunt Mae's.

I came back to school and discovered that my roommates had asked the housemother to move me out of my room. I wasn't the kind of person they wanted to live with. All my stuff was piled harum-scarum in the laundry shed, off the courtyard. The housemother talked to me kindly. She said she didn't make much of what they said, but sometimes it was easiest to start over. *They had no right!* I screamed. They had never said anything to me. *What had I done to them, what had I done to deserve this?*

The housemother moved me into a much nicer room for the same price. I shared it with one other girl, Darlene, whose friendliness invited confidences. Within a week I had told her what had happened. She said she was sorry, but really it was nothing and I would get over it. She had been a cheerleader in high school, and a virgin when one night half the team had raped her, then rolled her out onto her lawn. She had to be hospitalized. Everyone knew about it but nothing happened to the boys. Her parents didn't want to create a scandal. She had a little boy her parents were raising as her brother. You never would have guessed. I stared at her and I thought, *Everybody has stories and most of them don't count for much.* That's why we loved Maria Goretti. All the factors fell into place for her martyrdom; her death made her story perfect, the one we would tell over and over, knowing none of us could ever be like her.

. . .

I knew one place where they would want to hear my story if I told it with contrition.

On a Saturday a few weeks later, I wandered into a Catholic church near campus. It was cool and dark and empty, more than an hour before time for confessions. I sat in a pew near the back. I felt at home and I wondered why I had stayed away, when, if you thought about it, this was the only home I had left.

I had been angry with God for taking my mother from me, and I had defied God with my bad behaviors, but he would understand and his priest would forgive me. That was the very nature of the sacrament of penance. I only had to be sorry for my sins. I only had to examine my conscience and declare my guilt and my resolution to do better.

I never got past the most recent transgression.

Had I been guilty with those boys? I thought the answer was yes. Certainly I had put myself into an occasion of sin, going with them to their apartment, drinking their beer, lying in their bed.

Had I resisted? I thought the answer was no. I had been weak and submissive. They wouldn't have beaten me. They were too weak themselves. If I had mustered the courage and the energy to disgust them with screams and maybe some kicks and more flailing, their nasty little pricks would have deflated and they would have thrown me out. Instead, they did what they wanted, then spread my name around. That vilification had been my punishment. Sitting in church a few yards away from the confessional, I accepted it humbly, bending my head.

And the happy memories of my Catholic childhood faded, just like that. I can't say why it happened then, any more than I can explain a saint's vision. Why shouldn't sudden awareness, which we think of as bolts of understanding, work the other way, in the loss of knowing?

I stopped thinking of my mother kneeling with me or walking with me up the church aisle to the Communion rail. I forgot the cool touch of her fingers in my palm. I thought of her instead behind a closed door with her doctor. I thought of her in a car's backseat with someone who didn't love her, someone who pumped his semen into her and never saw her again. I thought of her waiting for a prince who never came, or came too late, or came but didn't take her away.

I thought of her naked by her window, mocking death at the door.

And I thought, If I have already made some of her mistakes unwittingly, at least I can choose my own from now on. I won't expect to be rescued by love or salvation. I was flooded with sorrow, but I thought, I won't be fooled by sentiment.

My guts cramped so painfully I bent forward, my head to my knees. I had not realized until then how much I wanted to make my way home to the Church, to its comforts and its promises. But if my mother wasn't in Heaven, why would I want to strive to go there? And if Heaven would refuse her, how could it exist?

I heard the side door open and I saw the priest enter the church. I knew he would speak to me and I would have nothing at all to say.

·TWELVE·

The years pass, and more people you love die, and you find you are getting old. One day you sit down and open the boxes that you have avoided since they came to you: the photographs and the letters, the prayer books and pages torn from diaries. You learn that although memory is a stubborn thing, sometimes it can be turned by patience and desire, and then you see things newly.

I began to spend time with my aunt and to talk about my childhood. We spent a weekend in the Texas Hill Country, and one evening in our room, I asked her what she remembered about those last months of Mother's life, about me and Mother, specifically. It was hard for me to get the question out. I felt foolish, at my age.

She squinted a little, as she does, as if she could look back if she tried hard enough, and she said, "'Course I was busy working and taking care of the little kids, but I tried to get over when I could. I remember that no matter when I showed up, you were in there on Edith's bed, reading or doing homework, sitting up beside her, or talking maybe, holding her hand. Once I walked in and you were brushing her hair with your fingers."

After that, other memories surfaced, one after another, and I began to write, slowly, for years, past the anger and grief and silence, back to my mother.

I CAME ACROSS a photograph from late summer 1957 and I have framed it and put it on my desk where I see it every day. In it, we kids are lined up on a vinyl couch with Mother: Karen, Joan, me, Michael. We are all languorous but a little glum, too, probably tired of the heat keeping us indoors. Nothing much is going on. Yet we are *together*. My legs are propped on a low table in front of us and I have leaned over to give Mother something. My other hand is propped against her hip. The intimacy is heartbreaking yet, in some slippery way, almost retrievable.

See? I think every morning when I look at it.

See how easy we were with her?

See how ordinary it was, just to love her?